Career Fulfillment Found

Take a Spiritual Journey to Happiness And The Career of Your Dreams

Jason Hyde

Career Fulfillment Found: Take a Spiritual Journey to Happiness And The Career of Your Dreams

by Jason Hyde

www.careerfulfillmentfound.com

Book cover designed by Night and Day Media.

<u>Dedication</u>

I am blessed to have two remarkable women in my life.

Their belief in me has made all the difference.

To my Mom Ellen, for your enduring guidance and support.

To my best friend and wife Bridget, for your love and care.

With all my heart.

TABLE OF CONTENTS

Introduction

"It is always in the midst, in the epicenter, of your troubles that you find serenity."

- Antoine De Saint-Exupery - Writer

As I look back, 2006 was the most difficult year of my life. My wife and I desperately wanted to have a baby but we were having trouble conceiving. 'Why wouldn't God want me to be a Dad?' I thought. I wanted so badly to be successful at work and make a lot of money, but I felt as if I was falling short. 'How could I possibly work any harder?' I wondered. I wanted life to be awesome and I had no idea how to move things faster in order to get what I wanted. All of those things led to tremendous strain at home as well. I was 35 years old and it felt like absolutely nothing was going right.

Then one day when I was feeling particularly lost, I stumbled upon some information on the Law of Attraction that truly helped me to step outside of my foggy head for a moment. It allowed me to gain an understanding about why I was in a difficult place. After all, even the best mechanic in the world can't fix a car while driving it.

When I say "stumbled upon" information, I should acknowledge that I no longer believe in coincidences. The saying "When the student is ready, the Teacher will appear" has always fascinated me. It's attributed to

Buddha. My experience has taught me that the Teacher can be just about anyone or anything. The Teacher doesn't need to be a wise old Guru, wearing flowing robes standing on a majestic mountaintop, or a spectacled professor wearing a sweater vest.

The Teacher can emerge anywhere at any time. It just happens that the "student" can't see the Teacher until that student is ready for the knowledge the Teacher has to offer. As students, we can learn from people of all backgrounds, particularly children. Teachers can also take the form of books, sentences, or perhaps even just single words, like "surrender," which we'll discuss later. A Teacher can be something found in nature too.

The Law of Attraction became my entry point into the world of self improvement. Everything I learned about self improvement would somehow lead to something else I was supposed to learn. I began to "stumble upon" Teacher after Teacher and I devoured all of the information I could. I consumed everything from Spiritual teachings to more emotional and psychological knowledge. I am still an avid student of self improvement information. It's an area that I am passionate about and find completely fascinating.

Over the next 6 years, my life did seem to get much better. Because I changed, so did my circumstances. My marriage was great. My wife and I welcomed two beautiful sons into our lives. My business as a Financial Advisor grew, despite the worsening economy; and to further my personal and career growth, I took a new position with another company.

By 2012, I should have been on top of the world, but I wasn't. Despite all of the self-improvement information

I had absorbed, and the fact that my life was where I thought I wanted it to be, I continued to feel trapped by anxieties, doubting my capabilities and often neglecting those closest to me – my beautiful wife and sons.

Then in the middle of the night on July 17th 2012, I was awake with insomnia. But that night, instead of watching something completely pointless on TV, I chose to check out some You Tube videos of spiritual teacher, Dr. Wayne Dyer. (Again, when the student is ready, the teacher will appear.)

Something Dr. Dyer said that night gave me a tremendous amount of clarity and I saw a very clear pattern in my life. Oprah would call it an "a-ha moment". In order to capture this new understanding, I began to write.

I realized my career, while financially rewarding for the most part, had really been a major source of fear, anxiety and even despair. This pressure gave me sleepless nights and a long-term prescription for anti-anxiety medication. Frustration with my career was clearly the reason why I wasn't able to enjoy life fully and be grateful for what I had. I wasn't able to see all of the wonderful things in my life and just be happy.

Despite being a hardworking, dedicated professional, striving for success at work had been a never-ending fight. I finally saw that I was always struggling to create significance and certainty in my career but I never felt as if I was getting there. The fight was exhausting. I mistakenly believed that once I finally obtained the successful career I was striving for, as though it was some sort of destination, then I would be happy. But I was wrong. It felt as though I was running in quicksand every day.

What Dr. Dyer said enabled me to understand my struggle with career fulfillment and happiness in general. It was a quote from Buddha.

'There is no way to happiness; happiness is the way.'-
Buddha

That quote was very powerful for me. It helped me understand that happiness, as well as a successful career, are *not destinations.* Happiness and success are states of being. There is no way to experience happiness and success without actually being happy in the present.

Over the course of the next several months I was dedicated to writing and finding answers. I called upon the lessons I had learned over the previous 6 years to discover how to have, keep and maintain a fulfilling career and a happy life.

In order to find those answers I had to unravel the myriad of emotions and mindsets that had affected my attitude towards my career. I needed to understand why I hadn't experienced a truly fulfilling career before. I also needed to uncover what having a fulfilling career meant to me - the true me.

I found myself on a journey to understanding. It was a truly spiritual journey that would ultimately carry me to career and life fulfillment and happiness. It helped me understand that I am unique, talented and capable. I possess gifts that are exclusive only to me. I just needed to find those gifts. I was also able to recognize that my gifts were much closer than I had ever realized before.

You have the same uniqueness and gifts.

ABOUT THIS BOOK

Writing about my spiritual journey to fulfilment and happiness in work and life has taught me so much, I wanted to share it. That is the foundation for this book. In researching and writing it, I have spoken with many other men and women who, like me, were at a crossroads or a dead end in their work lives and often in their personal lives. Their stories were often similar to mine and their pain became my pain.

In addition to the experiences and understanding I will be sharing throughout this book, I have also included exercises that will be of value to you, along with a separate workbook that you can find on the website www.careerfulfillmentfound.com.

I hope, as you take this journey with me, you will find the answers to create your own fulfilling career. I welcome your feedback and comments.

In the words of Anne Frank, whose own writing of her experiences during the Holocaust inspired so many of us:

> *'We all live with the objective of being happy; our lives are all different and yet the same'. – Anne Frank*

I believe what Anne Frank was saying is this: When you begin to uncover the true meaning behind what people want, it ultimately boils down to simply finding happiness. In that way, we may be different, yet we are all the same.

Now I invite you to take your own journey to happiness and career fulfillment.

I hope this book will be a "Teacher", for you.

Jason Hyde

Chapter One – What Does Work Mean To You?

BEGINNING THE JOURNEY....

"Oh you hate your job? Why didn't you say so? There's a support group for that. It's called everybody, and they meet at the bar." – Drew Carey, comedian

For those of us who graduated college when I did in the early 1990s, we were in the throes of a recession. Many people considered themselves fortunate to find a job, especially in the career of their choice. In my case I found a job right away with a major corporation in my field of Financial Services. I also had what I thought was a template to follow for success. My Father.

My Dad worked his way up the corporate ladder with an amazing work ethic and dedication to his company. He was my example. However, when I started my career, the paradigm for career success had changed. No longer was it easy or common for someone, no matter how hard he or she worked, to progress up the corporate ladder and retire with a gold watch and a nice pension. That paradigm has continued to change. Now, career success and happiness is much more dependant on having an entrepreneurial comfort level.

Today an entrepreneurial mentality, the driving force behind any healthy economy, has become much more necessary in order to achieve career success. Even in a corporate job one has to be much more adaptable and comfortable with a certain amount of risk and constant change. What we once thought were safe career paths are no longer safe. More than ever we are questioning our feelings about work and career satisfaction.

How do you feel about work? Do you feel truly energized when you get there?

More importantly, are you working to live, or living to work?

The workplace for many people is a pretty unhealthy environment. It causes fear in some, despair in others and just a general sense of malaise in others.

Today I feel positive about my work but there are certainly days when I don't feel as confident as I should. Sometimes the stress of a hard work week and the constant juggle to achieve a work/life balance can feel overwhelming. I force myself to direct my focus and energy in a positive direction.

Negative thoughts and emotions are too easy to come by and for most people negativity is their default outlook on life. Weeds after all, grow anywhere. Flowers have to be planted and cultivated and cared for. I am very fortunate to have recognized that the universe has so much to offer. We must simply learn how to harness its power for positive use.

Our attitudes about work and happiness have been influenced by our experiences and the environment in which we were raised. If we were raised in a nurturing and supportive environment, we will face even the worst day at work with more enthusiasm. If we knew from the day we were born that we were loved and supported, we would innately have a more positive outlook on life. We would automatically feel more comfortable with taking chances and expect to have success.

If our experiences and upbringing are negative it's much more difficult to believe that we will succeed. If negative thoughts and beliefs are left unchecked we won't even realize how capable we are. Many professionals have lost their belief in their true abilities. Some may exhibit negative habits which manifest themselves in a multitude of ways.

Others have been swept along in the fast-flowing river of society's dictates and expectations for our lives. Perhaps you have opted for a particular job because it's what your parents and those around you have always believed you were going to do. Perhaps you've chosen a career that is a family tradition. If you come from a long line of lawyers, for example, you simply become a lawyer. The same may be true for the profession you have chosen.

You might end up living for others, enabling them to live vicariously through you. That won't allow you to grow and fulfill your purpose unless of course, your purpose is in alignment with their wishes.

Your work life can often affect your emotional health but it can impact your physical health as well. If you have settled for a job, or more broadly, a career that is creating a drain on your well being, the results can be devastating.

These are difficult economic times. Some have been forced by economic circumstances to work multiple jobs (if they can find them) to make ends meet, support families and keep a roof over their heads.

I also recognize that some of you may be unemployed at this moment. My intent is to equip you with the means to escape from the detrimental effects you experience while out of work.

I believe everyone deserves more than having to settle for a regular pay-check or remain in a dead-end job. My goal is show anyone, who is interested, how to create the best career and life. Everyone deserves to be happy and fulfilled. My main reason for creating this book is to help you get there.

Your Career Outlook Today

Before we start to fix things, we need to figure out what exactly is broken. For a moment think about your current or most recent job and how you feel about it. Which one of the following statements most closely matches how you feel about that job and current career prospects?

a) It's a true vocation; it is a true joy. It doesn't feel like work but is a fulfilling environment that allows me to grow.

b) It's OK, I get along with my colleagues and at least it's keeping the wolves from the door. It can be stressful but I am grateful to have a job these days after all.

c) It pays the bills.

d) The thought of working makes me literally sick. I've taken significant time off work due to work induced stress this year.

e) I feel so unfulfilled. I know there's something more out there for me. I wish I could find a job I love. I feel like I'm wasting my life and living for weekends and vacations (which I can't even afford to go on!)

Which of those statements most closely represents your feelings? Because you are reading this book, my guess is that your answer falls within responses c) to e). Let's take a look at each of those.

It Pays the Bills (C)

You may view work as no more than a 'necessary evil' that pays your bills. Your job leaves you resembling a robot, lacking all emotion, responding to instructions and simply going through the motions of life.

Your emotions are probably buried so deep you don't even know where to begin to dig them up. You find yourself automatically responding to the chiming of the clock which marks the passing of the hours.

Your day is comprised of a monotonous routine of waking up, going to work, carrying out your job and returning home to family commitments or the responsibilities of maintaining a home. Each day is the same with the exception of weekends where life seems to slip into oblivion with more domestic or family responsibilities.

You deserve more than that. The universe wants to help you. You need to reach out and begin to create the career and life you deserve. You deserve to be happy and fulfilled in your job, and this book was created to help you get there.

The Thought of My Job Makes Me Ill (D)

We may say these words in jest occasionally, but for some people, thinking about their job and having work induced stress is far from humorous. Here's a frightening statistic about today's worker. I was shocked when I read it.

In March 2012, the *Huffington Post* revealed that up to one million Americans skip work every day [1] due to stress. Three out of four of those surveyed reported that their work was stressful. A quarter of all of those questioned cited their job as the most stressful thing in their lives.

Perhaps you or someone close to you is currently suffering from extreme stress that brings you to the verge of tears at the slightest provocation. Have you recently been prescribed anti-depressants or anti-anxiety medication by your doctor? Are you having trouble sleeping? Are you crying behind your newspaper on the daily train commute or in the parking lot when you reach work?

Some stress may be considered positive such as responding to short term deadlines to complete a project and earn a bonus. Chronic long-term stress is a completely different ballgame. Prolonged periods of stress can lead to long term health conditions such as diabetes and heart disease. The more stressed we are, the more likely we are to resort to habits that aren't good for us, such as binge drinking, comfort eating, chain smoking, drug use, or even watching countless hours of stupid television. As we seek an escape in the hazy blur of a surreal world, the return to reality becomes more and more difficult to face and self-destructive habits can become the norm.

Long-term stress also exacerbates feelings of low self-esteem. This is a serious matter and above all identifies why we need to reframe our way of looking at life. We must unravel the negative habits we've learned and call on the Universe to work with us as we create a whole new world for ourselves.

I Feel So Unfulfilled (E)

Perhaps for you, particularly in today's economy, there are mitigating circumstances for your sense of feeling unfulfilled at work. Perhaps you were in your dream job, or working towards a long term career goal but your job was eliminated. In these difficult economic times you may have taken what you regard as a short term solution to keep your head above water.

That's OK. Many of us find ourselves at some point in our careers in a job that we know is not where we were meant to be. It may feel like a downward step but it's not. It's nothing to be ashamed of but rather a matter of temporary survival.

Maybe your career hasn't crash landed because you are struggling to get it off the ground. You may be one of the many highly qualified graduates having difficulty securing a role that reflects your skills, finding yourself 'underemployed' and working at a job you can't stand simply to make ends meet.

You may be working for a company that expects ever increasing responsibilities with no corresponding increase in your salary. Are you living under the constant threat of job losses within your company? Are your bonus targets gradually increasing as your client base gets smaller?

Or perhaps you are just plain bored and you feel like your precious time is being eroded away in your menial and pointless job. Weekends and evenings offer a solitary temporary respite and vacations represent a ray of light on an otherwise gloomy horizon.

And of course any reason why you may feel unfulfilled with your career will not be helped in the presence of excessive financial stress. Too many workers settle for whatever job they have because they feel handcuffed by the "30 day monster," their monthly bills.

> *"Why is there so much month left at the end of money?" - John Barrymore – Actor*

Based on the statistics mentioned above, with three out of four Americans considering their jobs stressful, one thing you can be certain of is that you are not alone.

A Note on Complacency (B)

Before we continue, I want to address anyone who happened to agree with answer b) above. Where your job is just OK? You don't love it but it doesn't make you sick.

If that's the case, my guess is that you're probably kidding yourself or you're at risk of slipping into complacency. You definitely aren't in your dream job but you've probably convinced yourself that your job is good enough. Why bother trying to strive for more?

With that attitude you definitely won't rise higher than your current situation. It's called a 'self-fulfilling prophecy'. You tell yourself you aren't destined for a better career so you make no attempt to improve it, and allow life to happen to you. Your decision is therefore justified.

I believe that you deserve so much more and you should too.

If you choose to remain in your situation, that is your prerogative and I respect your decision but I believe you're here for more than that. Before you shrug indifferently, you're obviously reading this book for a reason so there is an inner voice that's urging you to do something differently. That voice is telling you that you're not fulfilling your life's purpose.

As you read on, I hope you listen to that inner voice. It's there for a reason.

The Universe Wants You to Be Happy

A variety of reasons exist for your lack of career fulfillment but ultimately what each of us wants boils down to the same thing. We are all seeking what seems to be a continually elusive feeling of happiness.

Even when we do find happiness, it can feel very fleeting. After all, happiness is not a *permanent* state of being. It is not possible to be constantly happy. The goal is to make happiness your new normal; your default outlook on life.

Happiness is waiting for you, not in the distant future, conditional on some vague premise. It is not a limited resource with each individual allocated a specific lifetime amount. Nor is it restricted to members of some exclusive esoteric club that you haven't joined.

Happiness is infinite and it is abundant and it is available to you. This is the big secret that began to turn everything around for me. It will for you too. *Happiness is not a destination.*

We don't wait until we achieve a goal or reach a milestone to be happy. We have to "live happy" first. We must BE content, BE grateful, first.

So now you might be saying "Yeah right! This guy has no idea what I've been through! I'm dealing with _____ and I have to put up with _____ and on top of that I still have to _____!"

Can you fill in any of those blanks? Just relax a minute. I believe that I have figured this out and I can help you. I truly believe once you understand the rules, and gain a better perspective, you can turn things around and actually BE happy in no time at all. That will be the starting point on your path of career fulfillment.

I've experienced times when thoughts of what was wrong and difficult were so prevalent it never even occurred to me that happiness was right in front of me all along. I'm here to help you to reach the point where you have a fulfilling career. I'll also throw in a happy life as an added bonus. Regardless of your circumstances today, I believe I can take you to a better place in your job and your life.

What I Have Discovered About Happiness

When you're happy you are fulfilling your purpose in life and you are on the right path for your soul. You will be immersed in the positive, life giving energy of what is referred to as 'the flow'. The flow of happiness will carry you serenely along the right path for your life. You will no longer be fighting the current of a raging river with negativity; you will float along the river of your life on a raft of happiness.

Happiness is also about the divine. To you that may be God, your own individual higher power or Source. Whatever the divine is for you, happiness connects you to your higher power and you must be in harmony with your higher power in order to achieve career fulfillment.

Are you willing to give happiness a chance, knowing that it has the potential to lead you to the career you dream of? Even if you are terrified to let go while you are fighting against the current of your life, isn't it worth a try? You may be familiar with the saying "if you always do what you've always done, you'll always get what you've always gotten." Your results will not change if you don't change. You'll remain in that place of negativity and may never attain the career fulfillment that you deserve.

Before we begin our next chapter, here is an exercise that can provide valuable insights.

In other chapters, you will find exercises like the one below designed to stimulate your thoughts and elicit action. It may be useful to have a notebook and pen at this point. For your convenience, there is a complete Career Fulfillment Workbook containing all of the exercises you'll be going through available on the book website, www.careerfulfillmentfound.com.

Exercise 1 – Your Career Outlook Today

For the purposes of the following exercise, think about your current or most recent job and how you feel about it.

Which one of these statements most closely matches how you feel about that job and current career prospects?

a) It's a true vocation; it is a true joy. It doesn't feel like work but is a fulfilling environment that allows me to grow.

b) It's OK, I get along with my colleagues and at least it's keeping the wolves from the door. It can be stressful but I am grateful to have a job these days after all.

c) It pays the bills.

d) The thought of working makes me literally sick. I've taken significant time off work due to work induced stress this year.

e) I feel so unfulfilled. I know there's something more out there for me. I wish I could find a job I love. I feel like I'm wasting my life and living for weekends and vacations (which I can't even afford to go on!)

Where are you on that scale?

---

1 **http://www.huffingtonpost.com/2012/03/08/workplace-stress-1-million-americans-skip-everyday_n_1332172.html**

Chapter Two – Authenticity Will Lead to Work Happiness

*'Authentic empowerment is the knowing that you are on
purpose, doing God's work, peacefully and
harmoniously'. Wayne Dyer*

Are You Living Authentically?

When we refer to something as authentic, it means it's
real, genuine and with no pretence attached. Living an
authentic life means the same thing. Everything about
you should be real, genuine and without pretence.
Wherever you are and whatever you are doing, you are
yourself and no acting is necessary.

Authenticity enables each of us to reach out to the
universe and grasp all that is available. Learning to live
authentically is key to a fulfilling career and inner
happiness.

Do you feel there is a gap between the person you are
now and the person you can truly be? That certainly has
been true in my case. When I began my career as a
Financial Advisor I worked for a company that put me
through a training program in which I was taught how to
sell specific investments.

The training involved learning sales techniques I now
realize are used quite often in many sales jobs. I was
unfamiliar with them at the time. They're leading
techniques all structured to guide a potential client
toward an ultimate sale. The process felt very
manipulative to me. It just didn't feel right and it made
me uncomfortable.

I wanted people to become my clients because they wanted to and not because they were tricked. I wanted to work with people because they believed in me and because they could see that it was the right thing to do for them. The manipulative techniques I learned never worked for me because I wasn't being true to myself. I wasn't being authentic. It wasn't until I decided to try and *help* potential clients that my success as a Financial Advisor really started to take off.

To gauge whether or not you are living an authentic life, here are some questions to consider.

While at work do you:

a) Feel as if you're not being the real you. Are you parading behind a mask? For example, if you are employed in a team leader's role, are you sometimes more aggressive with your colleagues than is natural for you? If you're expected to be a team-player, do you suppress your feelings about ideas or projects because you feel that is how you're expected to be? Do you feel like you're hiding something?

b) Feel as if you have to be a certain type of person to fit in with your colleagues, like you're acting out a role? Is this because you believe that is how a leader should act or is that your personal experience of leadership from previous positions? Do you try to act like you care about your work when really, you don't? Or possibly, do you have a flippant or indifferent attitude toward work because you don't want people to think you actually care about your career?

c) Feel as if you aren't really being true to

yourself? Are you responding to questions and giving answers that you think other people want to hear? Are there times when you have some great ideas how to improve your company but you're afraid of speaking up for fear of ridicule?

d) Feel as though you have a number of different roles that you play within your working life. While you may be aggressive with your team, you may be completely submissive to your boss. This can all create inner tension.

If you have answered yes to any of these questions you may not be living your life authentically.

It can be exhausting emotionally to pretend to be someone you are not. It can cause us to lose sight of who we are. If you're not authentic you always need to be on guard. You have to work to remember who you are supposed to pretend to be in different situations. Living an inauthentic life poses a threat to your health, well being and financial security.

Symptoms of an 'Inauthentic' Life

You may be thinking, 'Sure, I may be pretending to be someone I'm not while at work but it helps me get through the day. Does it really matter? Don't we all do that to a certain extent anyway? It doesn't make any difference in my life, does it? Anyway, you don't know the people I have to work with.'

Being your true authentic self while at work will move you toward situations that are in alignment with what you were meant to be doing. I'll show you the steps to the career fulfillment you seek. Living an authentic life must be part of the process.

When you get home from work every day how do you feel? Exhausted, lethargic, or anxious? Maybe you're glad the day is over and ready to pour a glass of wine, put your feet up and watch some pointless TV?

Think back to an earlier section and the *Huffington Post* information about the number of Americans who skip work every day because they are feeling ill. I guarantee you that their working life is not authentic and they are suffering the consequences.

Here are just a few of the possible symptoms of living an inauthentic life.

- A need to take anti-depressant or anti-anxiety medication.

- Becoming emotional at unexpected or inappropriate moments.

- Smoking and drinking too much.

- Binge or comfort eating.

- Spending hours in front of the television or computer to escape the reality of your life.

- Spending time with your family but not being 'present' with them.

- Continually calling in sick to work because you can't face another day.

There is a way out from experiencing these symptoms.

Benefits of Authenticity

When we give ourselves permission to be authentic, we are free from negative influence. We are confident in our own decisions and actions instead of dependant on others' ideas and expectations for us. We can choose our own course in life.

Authenticity is a vital part of working in harmony with the Universe. How can the Universe help us if we are failing to live an authentic life?

In layman's terms, living authentically means being true to yourself. Your values will be your guide, rather than the desires of other people and external circumstances. It means being honest with yourself about who you are. You must be living authentically in order to be happy.

Here are just a few of the benefits of living an authentic life:

Increased Trust and Respect – You'll gain the trust of others and you'll trust yourself as well. People are instinctively drawn to and respect those who are authentic.

Integrity – Authenticity automatically aligns you with your true core values.

Confront Problems Head On –You will have the courage to confront issues within your life. Rather than burying your head in the sand you'll resolve issues quickly.

Increased Self-Esteem – Knowing who you are and

following your core values will lead to an increased confidence in all areas of your life, particularly your career. You'll have the quiet confidence that can only come from being your true self.

Reduced Stress – Authenticity is liberating. Think about how much better it will feel not to have to think about how to behave. Reduced stress from authenticity will also lead to harmony in so many other areas of your life.

Realizing Your True Potential – Living authentically will ultimately enable you to set out along the life path you were destined for. It will enable you to do what is right for you.

Let's try a brief exercise now to stimulate your mind about authenticity in the workplace. If you find that you have not been true to yourself in the workplace, or in your life over all, that's fine. You are certainly not alone. In the next chapter we will look at a concept that may show you the reason why you have not been authentic. You just don't realize who *you* truly are yet.

Exercise 2 – What Type of Position Suits Me?

Part One – Can Be

Take some time completely alone. For a time of true reflection I recommend a half an hour with a pen and notebook. This may be a challenge to some of you if you're not accustomed to sitting still or actually facing the inner you.

Think of words that reflect who you can be in your life, as it relates to your career. In **Appendix A** you'll find suggestions to stimulate your thought processes relating to both specific job skills and also personal characteristics. We need both 'hard' and 'soft' skills to carry out any job successfully. You may find it useful to circle any words you feel are examples of who you *can be*, given the opportunity and the right career path.

Combine the words in the appendix with thoughts of your own. I believe this will begin to help you understand the type of career that is right for you.

Part Two – Currently Are

Once you've completed part one and circled or written down those words that reflect who you feel you can be in a work environment, you can move on to the next part of this exercise. This is the time to face up to the reality of your current situation so you can begin to turn it around.

Think about your current or most recent job. Now place a check next to every single word you've circled which is a characteristic you are *currently demonstrating* in that job.

Be honest, how many of those words that you've circled - the words that you know are the truth about who you can be – have you placed a check next to?

If you have not checked many of your circled words, you aren't authentic at work, which may possibly extend to life outside of your working environment as well.

Chapter Three – Uncovering the REAL You

"You find peace not by rearranging the circumstances of your life, but by realizing who you are at the deepest level." - Eckhart Tolle

Who are you? Really!

You are now ready to move on to the next stage of your spiritual journey. In the previous two chapters you uncovered patterns regarding your career. You understand the thoughts, feelings and actions that have kept you stuck in an unfulfilling career until now. You know what your previous overall outlook toward your career was and whether or not you have been your authentic self while in the work environment. It is important to understand what your history has been so that you can move forward.

"Those who cannot remember the past are condemned to repeat it." – George Santayana

If your career has been unfulfilling, you certainly don't want history to repeat itself. Knowing where you have been, with regard to career fulfillment, is only part of what you need to know to avoid slipping back into old patterns and habits. You now need to have a true understanding of *why* you were stuck in an unfulfilling career in the first place.

A great place to start is to understand who *you* really are. After all, if you don't really understand who *you* are, how can you know:

- Why *you* were stuck?

- What *you* want your career to be?

- The best way for *you* to get there?

In order to find out who you truly are we are going to grapple with an unusual concept – **the ego versus soul.**

Ego versus Soul

To set yourself free and to accept all the Universe has to offer, it is crucial for you to understand that there are two completely different parts of 'you', the ego and the soul. Once you understand that, you can begin to make changes in your life that will lead toward the career fulfillment you long for.

Ego – A Brief Definition
No matter who you are you have an ego. Some of us are more controlled by our ego than others.

The dictionary definition of 'ego' is:[1]

1. The self, especially as distinct from the world and other selves.

2. In psychoanalysis, the division of the psyche that is conscious, most immediately controls thought and behavior, and is most in touch with external reality.

   a: An exaggerated sense of self-importance; conceit.

   b: Appropriate pride in oneself; self-esteem'.

The word ego may cause you to imagine a person filled with pride, who regards himself or herself as 'king or queen of the roost' or the 'top dog'. You may also think of that person as rather arrogant with an inflated sense of self-esteem. I'm sure none of us have to think too hard to bring someone to mind within our social circles or working environment that fits that description.

Everyone's ego is firmly rooted in the world around us. The world we can see and touch. The ego seeks to control who we are, through our thoughts and behaviour. It also causes us to identify ourselves with who we are in the external world, as in what job we do and what material possessions we have.

The ego craves attention. It can't cope with simply being 'ordinary', it needs to be noticed. It needs to be important or needed. Once the ego has experienced the illusion of importance, accomplishments and material possessions, it seeks more of the same.

At its worst, the ego is ruthless. If we only live our lives based on what our ego would have us believe, we would live in a spirit of self-centeredness, seeking everything only for ourselves and focusing on personal gain.

Our ego is the voice that speaks most strongly in our heads because it is driven by what we can see in the world and encouraged by subliminal messages we are constantly receiving. Think about billboard advertisements urging us to buy a new car or marketing campaigns that craftily convince us that if we could only lose weight, buy the right clothes or purchase some celebrity's latest brand of perfume we would have the perfect life.

How do we know when our ego is in control of our thoughts, feelings and actions?

Think back to the last time you were upset, irrational or angry with someone (even yourself). Think back over the truly rash decisions or big mistakes you've made in your life. That's your ego talking!

The Soul

The soul is the true you, the authentic part of you; the spiritual self, connected to the whole world and all that is beyond the world we see. It isn't easy to describe the 'soul' in one or two sentences.

While the voice of the ego feels like it is speaking through a megaphone and drowning out everything else around it, the voice of the soul is a 'still, small voice' inside – a voice of reason.

The soul has its essence in a divine source, a higher, spiritual realm, whatever form that may take for you. It will mean something personal to each of us, whether we follow a particular religion or not.

The soul belongs to something greater, something that connects all of us with the Universe and each other. People who live in harmony with their soul understand that the happiness available from the Universe cannot be exhausted and there is no time limit to accept the abundance that is offered. They are at peace with themselves and it is reflected in everything, including their career. Rather than relying on what their ego is telling them, they trust the divine and follow their Soul's path, taking advantage of the Universe and all of its abundance.

Entire books have been written on the subject of the dual existence of the ego and the soul within us all, but the most succinct explanation I have found is from a blog post written by author and spiritual teacher Dr. Wayne Dyer.

He explains the tension between the ego and the soul as follows:

"No one has ever seen the face of ego. It is like a ghost that we accept as a controlling influence in our lives. I look upon the ego as nothing more than an idea that each of us has about ourselves. The ego is only an illusion, but a very influential one. Letting the ego-illusion become your identity can prevent you from knowing your true self. Ego, the false idea of believing that you are what you have or what you do, is a backwards way of assessing and living life.

You've probably noticed the word AMBULANCE written backwards on the front of a vehicle so that a person seeing it in their rear-view mirror can read it. When you look into a mirror, what you see is backwards, too. Your right hand is your left, your eyes are reversed. You understand that this is a backward view that you are seeing and you make the appropriate adjustments. You do not confuse reality with the image in the mirror.

The ego-idea of yourself is very much like the mirror example, without the adjustments. Your ego wants you to look for the inside on the outside. The outer illusion is the major preoccupation of the ego.

The ego-idea has been with us ever since we began to think. It sends us false messages about our true nature. It leads us to make assumptions about what will make us happy and we end up frustrated. It pushes us to promote our self-importance while we yearn for a deeper and richer life experience. It causes us to fall into the void of self-absorption again and again, not knowing that we need only shed the false idea of who we are.

Our true self is eternal. It is the God force within us. The way of our higher self is to reflect our inner reality rather than the outer illusion. The description given by Sogyal Rinpoche in The Tibetan Book of Living and Dying is a wonderful explanation of this discovery: "Two people have been living in you all of your life. One is the ego, garrulous, demanding, hysterical, calculating; the other is the hidden spiritual being, whose still voice of wisdom you have only rarely heard or attended to." He refers to this hidden spiritual being as our wise guide.

When we learn to transcend the illusions sponsored by the ego, we can access this wise guide. We can invite in the higher aspects of ourselves to function in their natural, loving, and integrated design."

To simplify it further, you may find Appendix B to be useful. It shows examples of the differences between ego and soul, written by author and screenwriter Justine Musk. It can be a tricky concept to grasp at first but once you begin to understand, I promise you it will all fall into place and you'll finally have that 'Eureka' moment.

The Soul's Path

In order to experience a life of genuine happiness and a fulfilling career you must be on the soul's path. The soul's path is the only path that will lead you to true fulfillment. How do you know when you are on the Soul's path?

- You are fully aware of who you are.

- You seek and feel connection and love.

- You are infused by a sense of peace and well-being that no amount of money can buy.

- You won't need a checklist to tell you that you're on the right path, you'll know intuitively.

The Soul's path can not be gauged by perceived importance or status. No minimum pay check, allowing you to purchase more material goods, will be necessary to feel happy. No material object can ever lead to lasting happiness, contentment and a true sense of abundance.

The ego has an insatiable, unquenchable appetite. Feed it and it will only crave more. You only have to look around you to see evidence of it. Status, accomplishments and material possessions – by and for themselves, will only lead to more wanting of those things. The ego's desires never end. Has there been a time in history when people have experienced so much "success" and yet still feel so empty and unhappy?

Think about the world of celebrities. It's easy to bring to mind famous people who have substantial wealth. These celebrities are supposedly 'living the dream'. They may have achieved "success" by most people's definition and in doing so become famous. But if they have succumbed to the pull of their ego there is still a vacuum, a void inside of them and that emptiness is often captured by today's tabloid media.

Whenever we allow our ego to direct our lives we will never achieve true happiness. People whose lives are directed by their ego too often wait until the worst day of their lives to start listening to their soul.

The Ego and the Mask

Earlier in this book, I spoke about how many of us wear masks. Let's look at how one's ego can influence the use of masks.

'The mask acts like a defensive shroud to make the inner self invisible to both the outside world and to the self.' - John Pierrakos

One of biggest barriers to achieving our purpose in life and finding that elusive career fulfillment is the mask that we wear in response to our ego. We all wear masks every day to present the face to the world that our ego believes will suit our situation best.

Think back to the earlier exercise when we examined what it means to be inauthentic and the emotions we identified when we weren't being ourselves in a working environment. That is our mask.

We are usually not aware that we are wearing a mask because it is so much a part of our persona. Here are some common dangers of living behind a mask.

Living behind a mask can:

- Lead you to think that the way you are living is real and there is no other way.

- Make you insecure, seeking affection and approval from others and fulfillment from material things.

- Drive away creativity.

- Represses your soul, creating stressful situations and potentially long-term health problems (remember the statistics on the number of Americans who call in sick to work every day).

- Suppress painful emotions from our past keeping us from acknowledging and accepting experiences.

- Cause us to deny accountability for our actions.

- Shut out our soul – and God or your higher power.

- Falsely lead us to believe that without the mask our relationships, career and the very fabric of our lives would crumble.

For most of us, life without that mask is more than we can contemplate, leaving us vulnerable to insecurity, anxiety and feeling lost. At our ego's direction, we've worn our masks for so long we've forgotten who we are without them. The mask filters out everything that doesn't add to the goals of the ego, which includes the truth and reality of who we really are.

By simply recognizing the ego it will begin to fade, to make way for your true self. Once you recognize your ego you can begin to grow into the person you were always meant to be. Only on the soul's path can you achieve your life's purpose and discover what it is that you are meant to do and who you are destined to be.

At this stage of your reading, if you're beginning to realize some truth about your own life, I urge you not to become anxious. Instead take off your mask and listen to the voice of your true self.

> *'The real point of being alive is to evolve into the whole person you were intended to be'. - Oprah Winfrey*

By setting yourself free from your ego and following your Soul's path, you open the door to an abundance of blessings, including love, joy, peace, integrity, energy, emotional freedom, and creativity. You will be on the right path to fulfill your life's purpose.

As I have learned more about the ego versus the soul, it has become easier to recognize my ego as the cause of negative thoughts and feelings when they occur. I am now able to more readily recognize my ego when:

- I find myself worrying about what other people think about me.

- I have doubts about my abilities.

- I am afraid to try.

- I feel as though I am not successful in comparison to someone else.

And simply acknowledging that my ego is the reason for those thoughts and emotions causes them to dissipate. It allows me then to move my focus toward what is most important to the real me.

Listening To Your Soul

Author and philosopher Eckhart Tolle, in his book *Stillness Speaks,* describes the ego as a completely fabricated sense of who we are. The ego comes from and is fed by our daily insecurities. It doesn't want to let go even when we recognize what it is and how it functions. We can realize that we're being foolish about things we are thinking and feeling but still won't do anything to change. The ego clings to power because it doesn't realize that ultimately we come from God, and we are part of a greater whole and have no need to feel insecure.

The dichotomy of the ego and the soul reminds me of a snow globe. A snow globe is a small scene of some kind that is encapsulated in glass, filled with liquid and contains many tiny little white particles that act as snow.

When you shake a snow globe, it appears as though the snow is spinning and swirling all around the small scene. But then when you hold the globe still or set it down, the flakes begin to settle and the scene is clear to see again.

All of those tiny spinning, swirling flakes in the snow globe remind me of the thoughts and feelings caused by the ego. The soul is the peaceful scene you can see clearly.

So how then do you quiet your ego and stop the thoughts and feelings from spinning out of control inside of you? How do you get to the clear and peaceful scene that is your soul? Here are some suggestions.

Get in Touch With Nature

'All things in nature are not only one with themselves but also one with the totality. They haven't removed

themselves from the fabric of the whole by claiming a
separate existence; 'me' and the rest of the universe'. –
Eckhart Tolle

One way to get in touch with your true self is to spend
time out in the open. Escaping from the daily confines
of four walls will allow you to clear your head and listen
to your soul. Go outside to appreciate nature. And if
you can't go outside, then make it a point to look
outside. Be thankful for creation, for the beauty of all
things in nature.

Meditation/Prayer

By spending time in meditation or prayer you will find a
feeling of peace and open yourself to your Higher
Power. This can be done at night before you go to sleep
or first thing in the morning. It works best when you
turn off all possible distractions. Empty your head of
mindless chatter – which is usually anxiety encouraged
by the ego. The ego won't give up easily, but that's OK,
we're going to learn how to move beyond its objections
and focus on the positive.

If meditation is new to you, read the meditation tips in
Appendix C.

'By being peaceful, quiet and receptive, you pattern
yourself in the image of God and you regain the power
of your Source.' – Wayne Dyer

As part of that initial battle with your ego, try fifteen
minutes of stillness each day, ideally first thing in the
morning before you begin your work day. Find
somewhere you can be totally alone and just 'be'. Don't
say a word, just close your eyes and empty your mind.
When thoughts pop back in to your mind, which they

will, just acknowledge them and then let them go. Go back to the stillness.

I realize you have pressures you are dealing with and it may seem difficult to simply find a small handful of undisturbed minutes every day. It's just fifteen minutes and it may change your life. The only time for solitude you may find is in the parking lot before you head into work but that's better than not devoting any time to mediation at all.

Begin by trying it for a week. Take small steps. You can handle one week. If you find, as I suspect you will, that you feel better and the circumstances of your life have improved with less effort, then move on to a second week and then a month. After that if you feel that you can, progress to a half hour of simply being still.

When you quiet your mind, the noise of the ego will gradually be replaced by the calm, confident voice of your Source.

Keep a Journal

The psychological benefits of keeping a journal are well documented. It doesn't matter what you write. You don't even have to think about it. Simply take a pen and a notebook and find some time alone.

If you have not really written anything significant since you left school (apart from the occasional card and letter) the prospect of writing about emotions and thoughts will probably fill you with dread. Just remember, that's the ego talking again.

Why would the ego want you to write about your inner feelings and what really matters to you? It doesn't want you to explore your emotions or listen to your soul. It wants to keep you exactly where you are, firmly under its control in an unfulfilled life. Don't let it win.

If you're still not sure about keeping a journal, consider these benefits. Keeping a regular journal will help you to:

- Reflect on recent events.

- Clarify your thinking.

- Be honest about the way you feel.

- Enable you to connect with your soul and help you to intuitively understand whether or not you are on the right path.

- Understand where you may have made mistakes and how you can improve.

- Prompt you to ask questions about where you are in your life and where you want to go.

Some of you with an artistic flair may find it more helpful to use visual aids to express your feelings, such as photographs, cuttings, postcards or even your own paintings. Anything that will stimulate your creativity and encourage your thought processes is fantastic.

It's your own private journal, what you include in it is entirely up to you. Be natural and allow your soul to shine.

An Alternative – The Joy Journal

If you're not sure where to start with the writing process you may find it much easier to begin with a joy journal. It's much simpler for beginners because there are guidelines. You just write about what you are grateful for. As you begin to reflect on the joy in your life, your writing will naturally expand to include your emotions and everyday life. Simply write down activities and events of your day that have given you joy, where you've felt happy and fulfilled.

I'm not talking about escaping the office at the end of a long day. That's kind of inevitable. I'm talking about your leisure activities, time spent with loved ones, beauty you noticed, things that made your heart sing and your spirit soar.

If times are tough at the moment and rock bottom doesn't seem too far away, I understand it's hard to come up with positive thoughts. I'm telling you now; everyone has something positive in their life. Can you think of someone whose circumstances you would not want to contend with?

Here are a few prompts to point your mind in the right direction. It's a useful exercise to put you in a positive frame of mind:

Exercise 3 – The Joy Journal

- What makes you laugh?

- Think about the people who you love.

- When or where do you feel the most peaceful?

- Think about things that you celebrate.

- What are your strengths, what do people admire about you?

- What do you truly appreciate about other people in your life?

Now I'm going to challenge you! Write down at least five things that you have to be joyful about today. If you really can't think of five things write down as many as you can. You can come back and expand your list after we look at the importance of gratitude in our lives.

The moments that we're grateful for will be a key part to harnessing the full power of the Law of Attraction, which we will look at next.

You'll find this and all of the exercises in this book available in one document at www.careerfulfillmentfound.com.

---

1 According to www.freedictionary.com/ego

Chapter Four – Attracting a Fulfilling Career

"A man is but the product of his thoughts. What he thinks he becomes." - Gandhi

Using The Law of Attraction to Create Your Career

As we continue the journey toward happiness and explore your goals and dreams, it's vital that we understand how a certain Universal Law, most often referred to as the Law of Attraction, actually works. The concept has been discussed in countless books but most recently gained popularity in the book and video called *'The Secret'*. The Law of Attraction is the law that brings into each person's life, what they are thinking about and feeling.

The first time it really emerged into modern thinking was in 1906 in *'Thought Vibration - or the Law of Attraction in the Thought World'* by William W. Atkinson, an attorney, publisher, merchant and author who was a pioneer of the New Thought Movement in America. The movement believed in the idea of an omnipotent divine presence – God, or Source – and that all of us, without exception, are spiritual beings.

The Law of Attraction states that what you think about and feel will manifest itself in your life. Quite simply, positive thoughts and emotions bring positive thoughts and circumstances into your life and the opposite is also true. If your mind is perpetually dominated by negative thoughts and feelings, these will manifest themselves in negative circumstances in your life.

Unfortunately negative thoughts and feelings are where most of us spend our time. Think about it, when you go to bed at night what do you think about before you fall asleep? If we go back to the statistics on how work stress affects us, you can bet that most people reading this book will be worrying about their job or how to pay the bills.

By focusing, even subconsciously on the things that we *don't want* to happen, or *don't want* to do, or who we *don't want* to be, we inadvertently but automatically, attract negative events and circumstances into our lives. For too many people, negative thoughts and feelings are their default focus. Negative information and energy gets thrown in front of our faces all the time. Have you watched the news on TV recently? Weeds can grow anywhere, but flowers need to be planted, cultivated and cared for regularly. And you attract what you think about even if your thoughts are subconscious.

Understanding the Law of Attraction is so important because we can consciously choose what we think about and focus on. We can plant and cultivate and care for our thoughts just like flowers. By striving to think about the things we *want* to have, do and be, and feel the positive feelings that we associate with those thoughts, we will attract positive events and circumstances into our lives.

Personally I think that all of the books and movies you can find on the Law of Attraction are wonderful. As I mentioned in the introduction to this book, it was my very first step into the world of self-improvement and for that I will be forever grateful. But I also now know that the information you can find on the Law of Attraction generally will fall short of helping you achieve that fulfillment that you so desperately crave.

When I first learned about the Law of Attraction, it

made complete and perfect sense to me. I could immediately see how it had profoundly affected my life. I put it into practice and it was wonderful. But over time it seemed as though the practice of the law worked for some things, and for others it did not, which was frustrating.

Let me tell you why......

Most of the books and movies fall short of a complete explanation because they leave out a key component. They tell you that for it to work you must begin with the end in mind. You first have to ASK for what you want. Sounds simple enough and makes sense. But as we learned in the last chapter on the ego and the soul, what if you don't know who *you* are?

Do you want a new sports car? Do you want a fat bank account? Do you want fancy clothes to impress your friends and neighbors? In that case, according to most information available on the Law of Attraction, all you need to do is ask the Universe for those things. Then think positive thoughts and feel the feelings as though you have these things already and – poof! – they will appear!

If you are familiar with the Law and have tried to apply it, has it worked for you?

The problem is that thinking thoughts and particularly feeling real feelings that are not genuine to you is nothing more than acting. You can't fake your feelings and have the law work.

What all of these books fail to address is that your Soul,

the true you, really couldn't care less about most of the material possessions that are generally used as examples. They are all empty things that your ego craves. The ego is convinced that once you have them your life will be complete so you begin to believe that is all you need for happiness.

It doesn't work because your ego wants them for the wrong reasons. Its motivation is rooted in status and material possessions. Your soul, on the other hand is rooted in the truth, in love, connection and growth.

When I look back on my career, the main source of most of my anxiety has been my continual struggle to know in advance how my career is going to evolve and to create status. It was my ego speaking. The ego wants to be in control and be important.

The law will never work to satisfy your ego because your ego is not the real you and the Universe knows if you're faking it. But I do know with every fiber of my being that the law works. I used the Law of Attraction to become a Dad.

As I mentioned in the opening paragraph, in 2006 my wife and I wanted so very badly to have a baby and start a family, but it wasn't happening. It was a painful and gut wrenching time in our lives. When the Law of Attraction came into my life I could instantly see that the law had been working perfectly. It gave me exactly what I was thinking about and feeling, which was what I **did not** want. I did not want – to **not** be able to have a baby. That's what my focus was on, and that's what the Universe delivered.

So I changed my focus to what I knew I wanted. In this

case, that part was easy. I wanted a baby. I changed what I was thinking and feeling. I thought about and felt the feelings of how blissful it will be when I have my baby. I even spent time in the room of our home that was going to be our child's nursery, holding and rocking a teddy bear as if it were my child. It was so real to me I would thank God for the beautiful baby I held in my arms.

My wife became pregnant very soon after I learned about the Law of Attraction, and I continued the process of holding and rocking and loving that teddy bear for the 9 months she was pregnant. Then on August 1, 2007 I traded that teddy bear in for our first son.

I now realize that only God – or whatever divine source we place our trust in - knows the best path to achieve our desires and God will deliver the exact circumstances that we need *if, and only if* we are on the Soul's path.

If we are not on the Soul's path, and we are at the mercy of our ego, the circumstances and occurrences that God presents us with are intended to lead us to the Soul's path. Whether we choose to take that direction of course is up to us – and that is where our ego often gets in our way.

I believe that we as souls have been given this life for a reason and that we are all here to learn something. In Joel S. Goldsmith's book "A Parenthesis in Eternity" he describes this life as just a small parenthesis ( ) along the infinite path of our Soul's journey.

He writes, *"This should help us to understand that our present life on earth is only an interval in eternity. We*

have come from somewhere and we are going
somewhere, but because life is an unending circle, we
are again going to come from a somewhere, and we are
again going to go to a somewhere, and this will go on,
and on, and on."

Happiness and thankfulness is the Soul's path. Only
happiness and thankfulness will lead us toward more
happiness and thankfulness. A life lived in gratitude is
the only way.

> *'Be thankful for what you have, you'll end up having*
> *more. If you concentrate on what you don't have, you*
> *will never have enough.' – Oprah Winfrey*

Think back to that joy journal.

The purpose of our lives is to become more aware.
More aware than when we first arrived in this life; more
aware that we are truly here to be happy, and to
experience abundance and love and connection. We'll
never achieve this while we worry about what others
think or while we follow our ego's directions and seek
out everything connected with material wealth or status.

It can however be achieved by serving the greater good,
by experiencing connection, love, growth and
contribution. Those are the things that fulfill you.

When you decide what it is you want your career to be,
you can now use the Law of Attraction to your
advantage.

Dismantle Your Negative Thinking Patterns

It may feel like a very daunting undertaking to change

your entire outlook on life. After all, your focus has been on auto-pilot up to this point.

> *'Negativity is an addiction to the bleak shadow that lingers around every human form ... you can transfigure negativity by turning it toward the light of your soul' – John O Donohue, Anam Cara: A Book of Celtic Wisdom*

When I first realized that my own subconscious negativity was attracting negative events and circumstances into my life, my career and my entire life by extension changed immediately. I believe that by freeing yourself from habitual negativity, you can truly benefit from all of the abundance the Universe has to offer, and make full use of the Law of Attraction.

The first part of setting yourself free from negative habits is to identify them. You may not even be aware of how steeped in negative thinking patterns you are. Below are a few of the common ones that many people struggle with. Facing the truth can sometimes be painful, but the end result will release you from a lifetime of negative thinking and enable you to achieve the career and life fulfillment you seek.

How many of these negative thinking patterns do you identify with?

Life Stinks! - You think every single thing that happens to you is bad. You have nothing but negative expectations and don't expect anything good to happen to you. Ever.

That Stinks! – You'll decide what sort of person

someone is as soon as they walk into a room – and it's normally a negative judgment. You decide a situation is going to be a negative experience before it's even begun.

Nothing Will Ever Change! – You don't believe anything will ever change, for example, you've always had the same job, the same level of debt, never been able to buy your own house. It's always been that way, why should it change now?

Everyone Thinks I Stink – You assume everyone thinks negative thoughts about you before you've even spoken to them.

I Know 'B*ut*' – You know what you need to do to change your life and you are perfectly capable of it but you keep making excuses. You use the word 'but' too often.

I Do Stink – Whatever happens to you, you sink deeper into self-pity mode and blame yourself for losing your job, missing out on a promotion, a relationship break-up. Whatever it is, it's your fault.

You Stink – Everything that's wrong in your life is due to someone else's incompetence or inability to understand. You never turn around and look at yourself, after all, why should you?

Sometimes you may unwittingly adopt a combination of three or four of the attitudes above.

Negative thoughts are like a prison without bars. You can go anywhere, you can do anything, you can be who you were intended to be, but by wallowing in negative thinking, you just don't see that you can. You're stuck in the prison of your own mind because your negative thoughts cause an illusion that you can't, when really you can.

Circus elephants, when they are not performing are kept in place by tying a chain around one of their legs. The other end of that chain is tied to a small stake stuck in the ground. Elephants are known to be one of the smartest animals and they have the strength to knock over trees. Why in the world then, would they stay chained to a small stake in the ground?

Because they believe that they are stuck. When the elephants are very young they are chained to that same stake in the ground, but when they are young they don't have the strength to pull themselves free. After many attempts at trying, they eventually give up, no matter how big and powerful they ultimately become.

Can a fully grown circus elephant pull that stake out of the ground and wreak havoc on everything around it? Sure it can, as easily as you can break a tooth pick. Can you change your thoughts and improve your life and accomplish whatever you want to? Absolutely you can.

With one realization, one moment of clarity, you can begin to consciously change your thinking and in turn change your reality. Your life can be better in a finger snap.

How to Change Destructive Thought Patterns

If you've recognized yourself in one or two of the previous examples, that's OK. We all have them, it's part of being human. What you need to do now is use the necessary tools and begin to change them.

Here are some easy steps you can begin to take today to replace those negative thought patterns with positive, life enhancing beliefs about your life.

Acknowledge That Negative Thoughts Are There

Getting the opinion of a close friend or relative can be extremely useful here. So many of us believe that there is no problem with our attitudes, it's the world that has the issues and it's the world to blame for our frustrations and where we are in our lives. The reality is that it's our attitude that needs to change first, before anything else will.

Ask your friend for a candid appraisal of where they see you expressing negative thoughts or negative behavioral patterns. Be prepared to write them down. Perhaps after reading this book you already know some of them.

Notice When You Are Using Those Negative Thought Patterns

Try to recognize negative thoughts when they happen particularly with regard to your career. What are the triggers that cause you to feel anxious or hopeless about your career? Is it a particular task you are required to do or a particular colleague you have to deal with? Do you feel most anxious on the drive to work or when you get an email from a particular co-worker? Whatever your triggers are simply make a note of them when they happen.

Replace Negative Thoughts With Positive Thoughts

Each time you recognize when a negative thought enters your mind, replace it with a positive thought. Remember that seemingly negative circumstances can always be looked upon as opportunities for growth.

The likelihood is that your negative thoughts are a result of negative questions you are asking yourself. When you have a negative thought, look inside and ask yourself what question you are asking, and then flip it.

For example – you may ask questions like 'why do I have to do this awful job?' And you can change your attitude by changing the question to 'what lesson am I supposed to learn from this opportunity and how can I grow from it?'

Another disempowering question would be 'What did I ever do to deserve having to work for this jerk?' Instead change the question to 'what is this person supposed to be teaching me and how might I help them?'

Another question - 'how am I ever going to get all this work done?' could become 'what do I need to do to accomplish everything I am responsible for with the utmost quality?' Just like that – flip it.

Think about negative thought patterns as if they were a tall glass filled with a dark, dirty disgusting liquid. By changing your thought patterns consistently, instead of adding more dirty disgusting liquid to that glass, you begin to add clean pure water. Every positive thought is crystal clear water. And first it won't seem to make much of a difference, but over time the liquid in the glass will get cleaner and clearer until there comes a time when you won't be able to tell that there was ever that disgusting liquid in the glass to begin with.

Positive thoughts create positive feelings. When you consistently have positive thoughts and feelings, the universe will create miraculous and wonderful circumstances for you.

Can you see how beneficial using the Law of Attraction will be to create the career fulfillment you want and the happy life you deserve?

Chapter Five – Experience Happiness Through Gratitude

"Cultivate the habit of being grateful for every good thing that comes to you, and to give thanks continuously. And because all things have contributed to your advancement, you should include all things in your gratitude." – Ralph Waldo Emerson

Let Gratitude Lead You to a Fulfilling Career

Another way to put yourself on the soul's path and be open to receiving all the abundance the universe has to offer is to be grateful. An attitude of gratitude is also a key component when applying the Law of Attraction.

Searching for and concentrating on all we have to be grateful for leads our thoughts and therefore our emotions toward the right mental state to have a happy life. Being grateful will attract into our lives more things to be grateful for.

Gratitude is not a natural state. There are just so many things we can think about which could be perceived as negative. For most people their default thoughts and feelings are negative anyway. **Negative thoughts are the weeds that show up in any and every garden that is not tended to regularly. When you look for things to be grateful for, you are tending to the garden in your mind.**

The path to realizing your destiny is actually very similar to strength training. Think about it. When you're strength training in the gym, in order to build stronger muscles, you must lift weights. When you do lift weights, your muscles don't immediately get stronger. The first thing that happens after you have lifted weights is your muscle fibers are actually broken down. Muscles only become stronger when they repair and bond back together.

The next time you hit the gym you'll be able to lift the same weights much more easily than before. That's because your muscles were broken down and bonded back together even stronger.

The people you see coming out of the gym with toned bodies didn't start that way. They had to work at it. They broke their muscles down on a consistent basis and became stronger and stronger.

That's not so different from the obstacles we face on our own path to career fulfillment and happiness.

In order to achieve a truly fulfilling career we all have to face and overcome obstacles. Nothing we will ever find fulfilling is supposed to come easily. I have to imagine that you have obstacles that feel daunting to you right now. Facing down your obstacles can be painful and scary. But doing so will put you on the path of happiness and a fulfilling career.

Something you can do right now to overcome any fear you have about facing your obstacles is to put worry into perspective.

Why Worry?

'Worry does not empty tomorrow of its sorrow, it empties today of its strength' - Corrie Ten Boom

How many times in your life have you worried yourself sick over things you can't even remember today? For me, it's happened countless times.

What are you worrying about at the moment? Your

career is causing you concern, we know that. What else
is bothering you? How to pay the bills? How you're
going to meet the schedule you've got this week?

Think back five years. What caused you anxiety then?
How about ten years ago, or fifteen years? Do you
remember? No? I don't either. That's exactly my point!

In that case, wouldn't it make sense to think that the
things you are currently worried about concerning your
career are also things that one day you will have trouble
remembering too?

We're actually more likely to remember the nightmares
or scary moments we experienced as children than we
are to remember the obstacles that caused us to worry
as adults. When I was a kid, maybe five or six years old,
I vividly remember a fear that haunted me. I was afraid
that a "scary guy" was hiding underneath my bed each
night. If I had been logical – since when are kids ever
logical when it comes to frightening stuff? – I'd have
realized that no big scary guy would ever have squeezed
under my bed with all of the stuff I was hoarding under
there. That didn't matter!

What mattered was that I was terrified that the scary
man under my bed would reach out, grab my ankles and
pull me under the bed if I got too close. So at night
when I went to bed, I would flip off the light located on
the wall by my bedroom door and run as fast as I could
toward my bed and literally LEAP into the air before he
could reach out and grab me!

It may seem silly now, but at the time it was terrifying.

How does that relate to the obstacles that are causing you anxiety or worry today?

I believe that when this life is over for us, we ultimately return to God or the Source. From that place, on the other side of this parenthesis we call life, we will look back at the lives we lived and reflect on all the things that caused us anxiety as adults and realize there was never any need to worry at all. Just as there was no frightening man hiding under my bed as a child, there is no need for you to worry about the obstacles in your life today.

In this life there is no way we can ever fail as long as we keep moving forward and never give up. This life, including all of its obstacles, is simply a growing opportunity for our true selves.

Doesn't that help to put things in perspective?

Why We Should Face Our Obstacles Head On

Now you don't have to lift weights if you don't want to. You can *try* to avoid obstacles too. But if obstacles are actually opportunities for the growth you are supposed to be experiencing, it's got to be worth facing them. Right?

You may be sick and tired of obstacles and challenges. You are not the only one to feel that way. If Mother Teresa occasionally felt that way, then you are certainly allowed to as well.

"I know God will not give me anything I can't handle. I just wish that He didn't trust me so much." - Mother Teresa

If you're thinking that you just can't handle any more obstacles and challenges in your life, just pause a minute and answer this question. Do you want your life to continue to stay as it is today, or do you want change and growth?

If you want your life to be more, to be all that it can be, then you have to do the work and face the obstacles to get out of the hole you feel you are in.

Another question. Do you really believe that all of the athletes, entrepreneurs and successful people you look up to just show up having never faced any obstacles in their lives? Of course you don't. For example, take a look at the Olympics. Standing on that podium, beaming with pride, wearing any color of medal takes sacrifice and overcoming often insurmountable odds.

Think about any of the successful entrepreneurs who make the headlines. Do you think that they never had a bad day in their lives? Here are a few facts you may not know:

- Steve Jobs was fired from Apple at the age of 30.

- While writing her first Harry Potter novel, J. K. Rowling was a single parent living on welfare in a tiny flat having just lost her mother. What's more, that first novel was rejected by TWELVE publishers.

- US President Abraham Lincoln originally owned a grocery business that failed, resulting in his declaring bankruptcy in 1833.

- Automotive mogul Henry Ford filed for bankruptcy more than once on his path to global success.

- Creator of American Idol and American X Factor Simon Cowell experienced the insolvency of his first record label back in the late 1980s and was forced to start again.

- Walt Disney went bankrupt at least once before he finally established the now globally famous theme parks of Disneyland and Disneyworld.

"You may not realize it when it happens, but a kick in the teeth may be the best thing in the world for you."
Walt Disney

History is peppered with successful people who overcame the obstacles in their path to fulfill their divinely inspired purpose.

You may be able to hang on to a safe and stable life by your fingertips for a short while, but from what I've seen, life is going to throw obstacles in your way no matter what you do to avoid them. Everyone faces hurdles in their life, you only have to look at the examples above. If you carry out a quick online search you'll find countless more examples of people who overcame crazy and impossible challenges to fulfill their purpose in life.

Perseverance is the key. You are going to hit obstacles in your life whichever path you decide to take. Consider these questions:

Question One - Will you Take the Path of Least Resistance?

Are you going to try and take the path of least resistance? It *will* inevitably lead to challenges and hurdles anyway and still keep you trapped in your self-imposed life of choice. 'What challenges will I face if I take the safe route?' you may ask. Take a look around at your friends, your work colleagues and your family. Do you know anyone who hasn't faced some sort of challenge in his or her life? It may be health, the loss of a job, the loss of a home, the loss of someone close to them or the end of a relationship.

You might think this is proof that there's no point taking a risk because bad stuff will happen anyway or you may think that this is simply 'bad luck'. Have you considered that it isn't simply bad luck? Have you considered that it may be God or Source trying to shake them out of their self-induced stupor in an attempt to show them what their life purpose truly is?

Question Two – Will You Step Out on Your Own Divinely Inspired Path to Awareness?

Will you take the chance, knowing that there will be hurdles but confident that you will accept each one of these hurdles as a gift and an opportunity to grow? Isn't it so much wiser and ultimately more fulfilling to choose to continue to grow, learn and expand on who you are, knowing that the obstacles before us are all God-given growth opportunities?

You also have to consider the obstacles you try to ignore or avoid will reappear in another form at some point in your life. The obstacle is there because you need to learn that lesson. So if you try and avoid learning the lesson do you think it's going to just go away? And be warned, when lessons that you have avoided eventually come back, I believe they come back stronger and meaner than ever before.

You can't escape the inevitable but you can choose to learn, grow, evolve and step out onto that path of awareness. Facing obstacles will enable you to achieve your God given purpose in life and find happiness and career fulfillment.

Be Grateful for the Obstacles We Find Along Our Path

'Be in a state of gratitude for everything that shows up in your life. Be thankful for the storms as well as the smooth sailing. What is the lesson or gift in what you are experiencing right now? Find your joy not in what's missing in your life but in how you can serve."
– Wayne Dyer

When you're knee deep in the resentment engendered by your current career circumstances, it's difficult to feel grateful. I am sure you're shaking your head at me in exasperation once again. 'OK, dealing with obstacles, I can understand that, but this is a step too far. How do you expect me to be grateful with all of the crap that's going on in my life? My boss is a real piece of work (being kind), I'm behind on rent and I can't get out of this dead end job because there's nothing out there? You want me to be grateful? You must be insane!'

Below you'll find a list of some things that most of us take for granted every single day. Take a quick reality check. Think seriously about how many of these things you take for granted. Be completely honest with yourself.

How many of these things do you simply assume will be there every single day of your life?

- Food on the table

- A roof over your head

- Clean running water

- Your family

- Your friends

- Your job

- Your home

- Your health

Any one of these things could disappear from your life unexpectedly at a moments notice. Shouldn't we appreciate them all? What would your life be like without just one of them? How grateful are you that you have food on the table, family, friends, your health etc?

Gratitude is a matter of getting things in perspective which we don't always do when we're caught up in the melee and stresses of our everyday lives. It's particularly difficult when we're consumed by everything that's not right with our careers.

Start today to express gratitude for the simple things in your life. Try beginning this very moment. Fill in the blanks below.

"I am so grateful today for

1. my friends, especially (name)

   ....

2. the love of my family, especially (name)

   ....

3. the support I have from (name)

   ....

4. the people who bring a smile to my face (name)

   ...."

Are you beginning to get the picture? How does it make you feel when you think about these people? My guess is you are beginning to appreciate just what blessings you have in your life already.

When you begin to say thank you it transforms your whole demeanour and approach to your life.

Benefits of Gratitude

- Gratitude helps you to celebrate where you are in your life.

- Gratitude can help to dispel those negative emotions that blind us to everything positive in our lives.

- Gratitude helps us to handle stress more effectively.

- Gratitude increases our sense of self-esteem.

- Gratitude enables us to quit being obsessive about controlling every single aspect of our lives.

Remember we talked about negative thought patterns? Here's another tip.

Last thing at night try saying 'thank you' to your higher power for three things in your life you are truly grateful for. You can use the prompts above to focus your mind. It can be something as seemingly routine as the roof over your head, your health, your family or your children. It's so much better falling asleep with positive thoughts running through your mind than focusing on situations which only bring you anxiety. It may even be something that's happened during the day, an act of kindness from a colleague for example.

The next morning when you wake up, think of those same three things (or another three to increase that sense of gratitude). Include them in your Joy Journal or whatever journal you may be using to express your feelings.

If you make a habit of it my guess is you'll soon begin to feel much better. If it takes time, that's fine. It takes thirty days of persistence to build a new habit so note it in your journal as you go. Create your own chart for that thirty day period or highlight it within your schedule. Once you reach the end of the thirty days, you'll be amazed at the transformation in your thought processes.

Here are a few more of the benefits of gratitude for you to consider:

Gratitude will allow you to feel:

- A sense of quiet confidence.

- More joy and happiness.

- More sociable and outgoing.

- More forgiving and compassionate towards others.

- Comforted. You won't feel lonely, even when you're alone.

- More energized. The benefits to your health are immeasurable, your immune system is strengthened and your sleep patterns improve.

- Optimistic. You will be more predisposed to receive the good things in life because you'll begin to expect them.

So you must be most grateful for the growing opportunities that your higher power presents you with and see them for the blessings that they truly are.

Think about your own career. Think about the career path you have taken and why it's evolved that way. Has it been a deliberate career path that you've carved out for yourself, such as taking the relevant qualifications to enter the medical profession and moving from post to post in a steady ascent?

Or has it been a case of meandering and drifting from job to job, trying a few things and not really settling in any of them? If that's the case you haven't yet discovered what your purpose is. That's fine; you're now on the path to self-awareness which will help you to discover just that. The exercises you'll be completing will also enable you to realize what your purpose is supposed to be.

Let's begin by looking at the top five things you have considered to be obstacles or difficulties which have prevented you from achieving career fulfillment.

An effective way of doing this is to take a notepad and write down all of the jobs that you've had so far, recreating your resume in effect. For each job – or for your last five if you've had a number of positions throughout your career – write down:

- What you enjoyed about the job.

- What you really disliked about it.

- The reason you left.

- What you felt you learned from it.

We're looking to understand what may be holding you

back and identify any patterns that may have formed throughout your career. For instance, was it the authority you resented or just a particular boss? Did you feel you were overlooked for promotion? Were you subject to any discipline or fired from any of your jobs? What was your attitude toward your work?

What were the top 5 reoccurring things that you had considered to be obstacles or difficulties throughout your career?

1._____

2._____

3._____

4._____

5._____

Think back to *Exercise 1* which focused on what work means to you. To identify any negative patterns throughout your career ask yourself how you felt toward each job you've had. I've reprinted the responses below for your convenience:

a) It's a true vocation; it is a true joy. It doesn't feel like work but is a fulfilling environment that allows me to grow.

b) It's OK, I get along with my colleagues and at least it's keeping the wolves from the door. It can be stressful but I am grateful to have a job these days after all.

c) It pays the bills.

d) The thought of working makes me literally sick. I've taken significant time off work due to work induced stress this year.

e) I feel so unfulfilled. I know there's something more out there for me. I wish I could find a job I love. I feel like I'm wasting my life and living for weekends and vacations (which I can't even afford to go on!)

If you find that responses (c) to (e) keep cropping up as frequent answers, this suggests to me that you are caught up in the negative thought patterns I discussed earlier. This is why it's so important to begin to express gratitude in your life to turn those negative thought patterns around and attract positive events into your life. If you use gratitude in your life on a regular basis, eventually it will become second nature. You won't have to even try to think positive thoughts any longer. It will just be your new normal.

It occurred to me recently that in this current economy, it's no coincidence we have an ever increasing number of "chronically unemployed." These are people who are not just out of work but happen to be out of work for an extremely long time. Of course there are unavoidable circumstances that can cause unemployment, but I have to imagine that negativity may be a key factor.

Negative thoughts are like being caught in quicksand. You've seen it in the movies when someone trips and falls into quicksand. The more they struggle, the more they sink.

The purpose of identifying your challenges and hurdles is so you can change your thinking about them. Just consider for a moment that these "obstacles" were actually an integral part of the perfect path to enable you to grow and evolve in this life. All of those difficulties brought you to this very moment and will lead you toward the perfect career for you.

Let's try reframing how you see these challenges to enable you to see them in a completely different light.

Like you, throughout my career I encountered obstacle after obstacle until I began to reframe all of my experiences and see them all in a more positive light. Ultimately, those obstacles became positive things in my life. Without all of those obstacles I would never have written this book.

Let's get back to those 'difficulties'. What if they were actually part of what you needed to experience in order to evolve into who you truly are - a beautiful Spirit that has been given the gift of a physical experience? If we assume that's the purpose of your obstacles for a moment, why do you think those obstacles are there?

Take a moment to think about what it is that you might possibly be able to learn from the obstacles you have faced and are facing now. How might these experiences actually be lessons and opportunities for growth?

For example, if you have continually come up against 'glass ceilings' or been passed over in your career there may be a number of reasons:

- You still have more to learn in the place where

you are. Are there any areas you can possibly enhance your expertise?

- You may be called to another career path. Perhaps it is with another company, or another career altogether.

If you have always found yourself working for difficult bosses:

- Examine your own attitude honestly. Are you simply allowing negative thought patterns to manifest themselves? We can only change our own thought patterns, not those of other people.

- Perhaps you have allowed other people to influence how you perceive yourself. Have you considered that having no boss at all might be the best option for you – i.e., setting up your own business?

Now write down the most likely reasons why you came across the top 5 obstacles you listed earlier. What were you supposed to learn? Did you learn from those obstacles already? Can you learn from them now?

1._____

2._____

3._____

4._____

5._____

We have to realize that we must be grateful for every single experience we're living through and the circumstances that we are facing today. Likewise, we must also be grateful for all of the lessons we have experienced in the past.

Don't pretend the past never happened. It did happen and it's because of everything that you've been through that you are the beautiful and special person that you are today.

Embrace your past to its fullest extent. Appreciate the gift it has given you and the lessons it has taught you, all of it, no matter what you have been through. Source or God can use all of those negative experiences to transform you and lead you further along your path to awareness. Let me tell you something crucially important:

The greater your pain, the greater the steps you will take along your path and the greater your acceleration toward career fulfillment and a whole new way of being.

Appreciate the past. All of it, no matter what you have been through. That's powerful.

The opportunity to overcome obstacles is a wonderful thing. It allows us to work toward a place of greater comfort. Just like muscle must be broken down before becoming stronger, obstacles must be faced in order to grow. No obstacles, no growth. It's that simple. The good news is that there is a solution to every obstacle, often we just need to change our perspective. The obstacles we are presented with are exactly the obstacles we need to enable our Soul to grow.

As we move forward you will learn to equip yourself with certain tools that you can use to get yourself into the necessary state to achieve career fulfillment. There are internal tools, things that you can use to keep yourself in sync with your source emotionally and spiritually. There are also external tools that you can use to take specific action that will empower you mentally and physically.

Before we get there, now that you understand what has kept you from already having career fulfillment and why, and now that you have a better understanding of who you truly are, let's figure out what it is you really want.

Exercise 4 - Gratitude

Think about your own career. Think about the career path you have taken and why it has evolved that way.

Let's begin by looking at the top five things you have considered to be obstacles or difficulties which have prevented you from achieving career fulfillment.

An effective way of doing this is to take a notepad and write down all of the jobs that you've had so far, recreating your resume in effect. For each job – or for your last five if you've had a number of positions throughout your career – write down:

- What you enjoyed about the job.

- What you really disliked about it.

- The reason you left.

- What you felt you learned from it.

We're looking to understand what may be holding you back and identify any patterns that may have formed throughout your career. For instance, was it the authority you resented or just a particular boss? Did you feel you were overlooked for promotion? Were you subject to any discipline or fired from any of your jobs? What was your attitude toward your work?

What were the top 5 things that you had considered to be obstacles or difficulties throughout your career?

1._____

2._____

3._____

4._____

5._____

Take a moment to think about what it is that you might possibly be able to learn from the obstacles you have faced and are facing now. How might these experiences actually be lessons and opportunities for growth?

Now write down the most likely reasons why you came across the top 5 obstacles you listed earlier. What were you supposed to learn? Did you learn from those obstacles already? Can you learn from them now?

1._____

2._____

3._____

4._____

5._____

We have to realize that we must be grateful for every single experience we're living through and the circumstances that we are facing today. Likewise, we must also be grateful for all of the lessons we have experienced in the past.

Chapter Six – Determine What YOU Really Want

"All successful people men and women are big dreamers. They imagine what their future could be, ideal in every respect, and then they work every day toward their distant vision, that goal or purpose." - Brian Tracy

Goals Are Destinations

Another integral part to a successful journey is to have a destination. Goals are destinations. Most people don't set goals. They don't bother to ever take the time to think about where they want their life to go. They just meander through life and they are at the whim of external circumstances.

One of the reasons most people don't set goals of any kind is because they are afraid to make a mistake. There is an inherent fear in getting it wrong. After all, if they are not 100% sure of what it is they want out of life, why change anything at all? They think any change they make could be worse than their current circumstances.

Very few people are fortunate enough to know with 100 percent certainty what they want, particularly with regard to their career. But those who do go after it every single day.

I was never one of those fortunate few. And that was fine for me. Goals don't have to be perfect or permanent. Let's think about the journey of a large cargo ship that carries goods from one side of the globe to the other.

The cargo ship crew knows where the ship has been, it's departure point. The crew also knows where the ship needs to go, the port where the cargo must be delivered. The ship and its crew can't see the port of destination, but they know it's there.

The ship's captain follows the most efficient route available to get to the new port. There may be adjustments to their route which need to be made along the way but the destination is the same. But what if it changes? What if the crew receives a call in the middle of their journey informing them they are to take their cargo to a different port?

The same thing can happen with your career. If your career destination needs to change mid route you might kick yourself for not knowing you were headed in the wrong direction. You might resent yourself or someone else for wasting your time. You also might use the change as an excuse not to try to improve yourself in the future because your experience has told you that – it's just not worth it.

But the ship and its crew just set a new course and head in that new direction. Just like that. After all, the ship certainly was not going to deliver cargo to the same dock where it started from, right?

If you are looking for career fulfillment, then you know you don't have it where you are now. Even if you have to change your desired destination later, at least you moved on from where you know you won't ever find your goal, where you are right now. It reminds me of something sales coach Zig Ziglar once said.

"If you wait until all the lights are "green" before you leave home, you never get started on your trip to the top."

Also, how do you know you won't find your perfect

home on your journey to a different destination?

Figuring Out Your Goal

So how then should you go about figuring out what your goal should be? Let's start by looking at your gifts and talents.

Everyone is good at something and every single one of us has a unique gift, although we may not always feel that way. Our gift is normally something we enjoy doing. Something that makes time fly right by. Whatever it is, it certainly does not feel like work. Here are some prompts that may help you to identify your gifts and talents.

How Do I Know If I Have a Gift or Talent?

If you think you have a gift or talent (we all do!) consider for a moment how you feel when you're carrying out that particular activity. Here are some ways to identify your gift.

- My gift comes naturally and is effortless.

- I feel joyful and can't wait to do it again.

- Time flies by while I'm doing it.

- I feel completely fulfilled and a sense of being where I am meant to be.

- My gift makes me feel strong and as if nothing can stop me.

- My gift brings joy to others.

In the earlier chapter on ego versus soul, you learned the final statement is the most important factor to determine whether or not your talent is your God-given purpose. It will bring joy to others.

'You cannot be fulfilled without contribution' – Tony Robbins

If your gift or talent doesn't give something back, if there is no contribution to the greater good, then it will not fulfill you. It would simply be another example of the ego taking control in which case you will inevitably remain unfulfilled.

The Definition of Talent

The dictionary definition of a 'talent' is:[1]

- A marked innate ability, as for artistic accomplishment.

- Natural endowment or ability of a superior quality.

- A person or group of people having such ability.

A 'gift' (taken in the context we're thinking of) is defined as:[1]

- Something given; a present.

- A special aptitude, ability, or power; talent.

Our talents and gifts are something we're born with and they are specific to us. It will be easier to find your gifts and talents by thinking about how you might contribute to the greater good, instead of looking for gifts and talents that will benefit you. We all possess unique gifts that were given to us to make a difference in the world.

Choose Your Goals – Your Destination

The definition of 'destination' according to the Oxford English Dictionary is:[2]

- The place to which someone or something is going or being sent.

Or perhaps even more appropriate for our journey towards career fulfillment:

- The ultimate end or purpose for which something is created or a person is destined.

Have you ever taken the time to think about and write down exactly what you want your life to look like?

My guess is you are like most people and your answer is 'no'. Most likely you have spent your life reacting to the situations or environment you've found yourself in. You have been propelled from one event to another with very little planning involved. I believe that applies to most of us and I was no different.

We're going to focus totally on what you want now. Consider these questions and how they apply to your life. Begin to allow yourself to dream:

- What do you want to have?

- Where do you want to go?

And most importantly:

- Who do you want to be?

If you ask most people what they want, their natural reaction is to tell you what it is that they DON'T want, such as:

- I don't want to be broke anymore.

- I don't want to be unemployed.

- I don't want to be doing the job I'm doing until I retire.

They're thinking the wrong things and focusing their thoughts only on the negative. If they do have an inkling of what they want, it is only just that; an inkling. Statements such as, 'I want a better job' or 'I want a job that I don't hate' are generalist statements. They hardly qualify as being anything remotely resembling a destination if we look at the definitions above.

What happens to you if you don't know your destination before you set out? You'll be like that cargo ship, moving without purpose on the vast ocean with no real chance of accomplishing anything. You must choose a destination; otherwise you will simply be wandering around aimlessly.

"If you don't know where you are going, you will

probably end up somewhere else." – Laurence J. Peter

Now, I realize that thinking about what you really and truly want is uncomfortable. For most of us, our ego subconsciously tells us that we will never achieve what we want. Why would we think otherwise? Looking back at the evidence of our lives so far, there's no chance of us ever achieving what we actually want in life, is there?

Well I can promise you one thing. If you are not happy with your career right now, there is one absolutely certain way for that unhappiness to continue. Do nothing different.

> *'Insanity: Doing the same thing over and over again and expecting the same results' Albert Einstein*

You're breaking out of the road to nowhere right now. You're going to have a destination. No longer will you do what you've always done; you're stepping out along a new journey.

How do you find what destination is right for you? What should the goals be for your career? Let's figure it out now.

Play The Lottery? – Yup, Just Once

The first step is to go out and purchase one lottery ticket – just one! Yes, that's correct. I want you to buy a lottery ticket. No, I'm not crazy. I know that winning the lottery isn't the answer to career fulfillment.

I don't mean to encourage gambling and this isn't a time to be spending money frivolously. I know that as well as you do but $1 is a great price to pay for this type of knowledge and I make one promise to you now.

The purchase of this lottery ticket will pay for itself countless times over – but not necessarily in the way you automatically think it might.

The most wonderful thing about a lottery ticket certainly isn't the minute chance you have of actually winning. In fact, here are some scary statistics to put this statement in perspective:

Lottery Statistics

Depending on where you play your odds of winning the lottery will vary. State lottery odds are around eighteen million to one but lotteries across multiple states increase to one hundred twenty million to one! Those odds are incredible aren't they? Here's a more incredible fact. Around one in three Americans believe that their winning the lottery is the only way they will ever become financially secure.[3]

One in three!! That's a third of all Americans. How scary is that?

You are more likely to die from a lightning strike than you are to win the lottery. There are more gruesome statistics than that but I'm sure you get the picture.

The reason I am suggesting you buy a lottery ticket is because it buys dreams. Have you ever said to yourself or to your work colleagues, friends or family 'If could just win the lottery I would .....' and reeled off a list of ambitious desires? Things like buying a sports car, or traveling the world, or simply buying the perfect home or a vacation home on some desert island? Haven't you said that at least once? Of course you have!

Those lottery tickets buy dreams and those dreams can help us to figure out what we truly want in our lives and in our careers.

How does buying a lottery ticket help? It helps because we doubt our ability to actually achieve our goals on our own merits. But the lottery ticket is different. The lottery ticket offers the slenderest chance of what is (let's be honest) dumb luck – and our ego is completely OK with that.

What does that say about us? It says everything. It says that we believe we are more likely to experience ridiculous dumb luck then we are capable of creating the life that we want. Aren't you much better than that? That's a rhetorical question. Of course you are, there's simply no question to answer.

Now, I'm going to assume that you have your lottery ticket and we can continue with the exercise.

Think about how you would feel if the numbers on that ticket were the winning numbers! Now, allow yourself to dream. Close your eyes for a moment and really put yourself in that place of having just won the lottery. How would it feel in that instant when you realized you had no more financial concerns?

It is in this state you will find your desires for your life. You will discover your destination. Let's enter into that experience and create that list together now.

Exercise 5 – What You Want (Column 1)

Congratulations! You just won the lottery! Suddenly you're worth millions of dollars. From this moment on money and time and support are of no consequence to you. You can do and be anything you want!

That's awesome! Let's figure out what you truly want.

What Will You *HAVE?*

First we're going to make a list of all of the possessions you will *acquire (buy)* in your new found circumstance. I've provided a table below for you with four columns. I've got a feeling it might not be big enough for this list but it will do to begin with. You can complete this exercise in your workbook as well.

Now allow your mind to wander and dream. You're rich for goodness sakes. Forget people like Bill Gates, Warren Buffet, and Mark Zuckerberg. This is you!

Write spontaneously for a few minutes. Think about all of the possessions you've been coveting for your entire life. You can buy things for you and for others. It's all up to you. Just write in <u>Column 1 for now</u> but write, write, write, write, write, write, write, write.

Column 1	Column 2	Column 3	Column 4

Great, now let's move on.

What Will You *DO?*

Now, in the next table I want you to write down all of the things you will DO in your newfound circumstances. Remember, you don't have to worry about how you'll pay the bills anymore or who will clean the house. You are rich beyond your wildest dreams!

Again, write in Column 1 only.

What would you do? Would you travel? Volunteer? Start a foundation? What do you want to learn, where would you want to go? What would you want to do? Would you take flying lessons so you can fly your own private jet? Would you take a luxury vacation in one of the most beautiful parts of the world? It's your list and there are no right or wrong answers. We're on the path to ultimate career fulfillment.

Column 1	Column 2	Column 3	Column 4

Who Will You *BE?*

This may not be as easy as the last two exercises but it's the most important. In <u>Column 1 again</u>, I want you to make a list of the characteristics that describe you in your new found circumstances. If you're not completely sure what I mean, think about what type of person you will be. How will people describe you now? What will your career look like – or will it be careers? You can BE who you want to be. You have the financial freedom to choose.

Allow your heart to soar!

Column 1	Column 2	Column 3	Column 4

How Will You Spend Your *TIME?*

How are you going to spend your days now that you are rich beyond imagination, now that money is truly no object and never will be again, for the rest of your life?

You have complete freedom to spend your time however you'd like. Where and how will you spend your waking hours? Go ahead, in <u>Column 1 only</u>, write down your answers to that question.

Column 1	Column 2	Column 3	Column 4

Awesome!

Exercise 6 – (Columns 2, 3 and 4)

Feel - (Column 2)

Now that you have answered all of the questions in Column 1 for each of the 4 questions in exercise 5, we're going to return now to Column 2. Go back to the beginning and review each of your answers in Column 1. I want you to immerse yourself in the emotions of the reality of every single answer you've given in Column 1.

In Column 2, next to each one of your answers in Column 1, write down how each answer makes you *feel*. How does it feel to have all the things you've always wanted to have? How does it feel to do all the things you've always wanted to do? How does if feel to BE the person that deep down you've always known you were supposed to be? How does it feel to be able to spend your time exactly how you want to?

This isn't a quick exercise. For each statement, close your eyes; imagine yourself owning those possessions, traveling to those countries and being that person. Take time over each different answer. The more you feel, the more real those emotions will become.

This is really important so take as much time as you need with column 2.

Now we know the answer to the following:

- What you will have.

- What you will do.

- Who you will BE.

- How you will spend your time.

- How all of these things will make you feel.

Ego or Soul - (Column 3)

The next step needs some serious reflection as well. Particularly take into account what you learned earlier about your soul versus your ego.

For each answer in Columns 1 and 2, ask yourself:

- Is this something that my ego wants or does it come from my true self, my Soul?

- Is it truly God, or my higher power speaking?

- Is it something that is purely there to impress others, to prove something or create envy?

- Is it something that comes from a place of love, caring and a desire for connection?

- Does it benefit just you or the greater good?

These are tough, uncompromising questions and they require tough, uncompromising answers.

In Column 3, write down either 'Ego' or 'Soul/True Self' next to your answers in each row.

This exercise requires reflection and total and transparent honesty.

You may find it helpful to refer back to Appendix B before you begin.

Just remember, in the end it comes down to motive. If you're doing something that's purely selfish, that won't ultimately work for or contribute towards the good of others, it's likely your ego talking. If it's something that will help those you love and contribute towards the greater good in the world – that's your true self.

Yes or No - (Column 4)

Lastly we're going to use Column 4 to determine if you really want to keep each answer or not. In order for you to find the destination that will bring you happiness and career fulfillment, the things which will give you that success are the Soul driven things, desires and aims. The destination must be the answers that come from that divine presence within you.

So this is a simple exercise. Write down "yes" if you want to keep it or "no" if you don't.

That's it. Congratulations! Your list is now complete.

What you are looking at now is your first glimpse at your destination.

You know what you truly want and you know the emotions your true self, your Soul, values the most.

The destination for your true self is comprised of the answers you kept in Column's 1 and 2. The things you want to have, do and be, and the feelings they create within you show you the features you will find in the ideal career for you.

It may not be extremely specific yet, but it does give you a direction to move toward. It also gives you a compass by which you can make career decisions going forward. Any time you have a career decision to make you can ask yourself what answer will lead you toward the goals and emotions that will feed your soul.

1 Definitions taken from www.thefreedictionary.com

2 Definition provided by www.thefreedictionary.com

3 Statistics quoted here are provided by www.savingadvice.com

Chapter Seven – Internal Directions To Your Destination

"Success is 80% psychology and 20% mechanics." –
Tony Robbins

Now that you have an understanding of the destination that will fulfill your true self, it's time to start moving in that general direction. Over the next 2 chapters we'll look at the best and most efficient ways to get you to where you want to end up. These are the directions that will lead you toward your destination.

We are going to break down the directions you need to take into 2 separate categories. In the first category we will explore internal directions. In this chapter we are going to go through the tools you will use to prepare yourself for success psychologically. These tools will be the internal directions you will need to achieve your goals.

Have you ever known someone who was an extremely hard worker? Someone who put in more hours than anyone else they worked with? They made more prospect phone calls or went on more appointments or took on more projects? This is the type of person who works his or her fingers to the bone to try and become successful. But no matter how much effort this hard worker puts forth, he or she never seems to find success in comparison to their effort.

This person may do everything right mechanically to succeed at their job. They are just in a bad state mentally, emotionally and spiritually. And if you're not in the right state psychologically, all the effort in the world won't help. It's like running on a tread mill. Run as fast and for as long as you want, you just don't ever get anywhere else.

Perhaps you've also come across another type of worker, who never tries very hard but still seems to be successful. This person never arrives at work early or leaves late. They take long lunches and even make time during the work day to exercise. They're never stressed and have an air of confidence about them. Even though they don't put forth a lot of effort they still do better in their careers than most. The hard worker we mentioned before would most likely refer to this care free successful person as a "cheater" or "lucky" or most likely some other colorful words.

Of course effort is important, and we'll go over that in the next chapter. You have to take action. But effort is nowhere close to the importance of psychological preparation, your internal directions. You absolutely must be in the right emotional state to create the career you deserve.

Let's look at the tools you can use to put yourself into the right state so all of your efforts will not be in vein.

Step 1 - Surrender

The first step you must take on your journey to career fulfillment is to simply *surrender.* The idea of surrender isn't an easy concept for most of us. Society dictates that we take control and responsibility for our lives. If we have that ingrained in us, surrender is a difficult concept to grasp with it's connotations of giving in and weakness. But surrendering to God isn't the same as surrendering in your efforts to achieve a fulfilling career.

Surrender is actually a realization that to achieve our purpose in life we must accept that God has a plan for us. Accept that God knows what is in your best interest far better than you do. You've gone through obstacles and challenges because that is what you needed to go through for the advancement of your soul. You are exactly where you are today because that is exactly what your soul needs.

Have you ever heard the story about the man who was walking along the edge of a cliff and fell off? Just as he was about to plunge into the depths of a bottomless crevice never to return, he grabbed hold of a sapling sticking out of the side of the mountain. In his desperation he began to call out to whoever might be able to hear him.

"Help, help me please! Is there anybody up there?"

Just then he heard a booming voice that came out of nowhere.

The voice said, "I am here. I am God. Let go and you will fly. I will carry you."

The man was in awe having just heard the voice of God. Then he paused, thought about it and shouted "Is there anybody *else* up there?"

Surrendering to God can be scary, but it's a necessary step along the path to fulfillment. Be like water, not stone. Go with the flow like water and don't fight what is like stone. Don't fight the obstacles in your life that you have previously identified. Simply acknowledge and accept them. They are there for a reason.

If at first it seems like that stone within you is more

resilient than the water, I invite you to picture the Grand Canyon in your mind. That spectacular gorge has been carved deep into the earth, sweeping away everything in the midst of its overpowering presence formed over the course of six million years. Can you imagine that? Six million years?

Do you know what created that breathtaking landscape? Water; the stone was worn away by the water.

Don't fight what was, just accept what is. Surrender.

Step 2 – Ask For Spiritual Guidance

I have a question for you; when did you last feel anxious, fearful or lost? Possibly you feel like that now as you read this. Perhaps anxiety or fear has led to you pick up this book in search of answers.

Over the course of the next few day be aware of the times when your feel anxious. Thinking back to the very early stages of this book, you may be feeling anxious as you are traveling to work, when thinking about facing your colleagues or walking into the office environment again.

When I realize I am feeling lost or fearful or anxious, I stop and ask God to guide me. You might want to try this, it certainly works for me:

"Guide me now God. I feel lost but I have faith all that is happening is supposed to be happening."

Pause for a moment and allow yourself to connect to your higher power. Have faith and feel thankful for the guidance that you will undoubtedly receive.

Step 3 – Use the Law of Attraction - Manifest

'The power of intention is the power to manifest, to create, to live a life of unlimited abundance and to attract in your life the right people at the right moments'
- Wayne Dyer

Use the power of the Law of Attraction to bring into your life the events and circumstances that will propel you toward your goals. You know what you want. Now actively bring it into your life through your thoughts and feelings. Even though it may seem difficult to find the time to manifest, if it makes all of your efforts more effective, isn't it worth it?

I always do better when I have some specific guidelines to follow, particularly when I'm taking on something that's new to me. So here are some quick guidelines for you to follow to manifest the life you want every day.

- **Quiet your mind**. Take full deep breaths and then think about what you want your life to be. Picture yourself having, doing and being all of the things that you determined in the last chapter on destination.

- **Feel the feelings**. As you picture yourself having, doing and being all of those things, allow yourself to feel the feelings that you will have when they are real. Pretend they are real. Believe they are real. Allow the feeling to soak into you. Your thoughts and feelings send a direct signal to the Universe. If you feel those feelings, the Universe will make it so in your life.

- **Allow happiness and gratitude to flood through your body.** Be thankful for the blessings you have just imagined and felt as if they have already occurred.

- **Receive your new life**. As you begin to see this life you want and deserve come to fruition, simply accept it and be grateful and continue to stay in that place of gratitude.

Step 4 – Know That You Are Successful Now

"Success is the progressive realization of a worthy goal."
– Earl Nightengale

The Oxford English Dictionary defines 'success' as follows:

- the accomplishment of an aim or purpose: *the president had some success in restoring confidence*

- the attainment of popularity or profit: *the success of his play*

- a person or thing that achieves desired aims or attains prosperity: *I must make a success of my business*

What do those definitions have in common? They remind me of the ego and success being defined by external things we can't always control. They make no room for the Soul. Remember:

- you can't have a certain amount of money and suddenly feel successful.

- you can't live in that enormous mansion and

suddenly feel successful.

- you can't get that certain promotion and suddenly feel successful.

In fact, you can't get a certain **ANYTHING**, and then **BAM!!!** As if by magic, you are instantly successful.

Success is **SO** much bigger than that. Success is simply a state of mind. It's a feeling.

Look again at the quote above by Earl Nightengale. By that definition, in order to be successful, all you must do is consistently move toward something truly **WORTHY.** All of the things that you realized were your true goals in the last chapter are worthy goals because they came from your soul.

Any goal that comes from your soul is going to be driven by a desire for love, connection, growth or contribution to the greater good. Once you have achieved a worthy goal, in order to continue to feel success, you must have a new worthy goal and move toward it. The only place you will feel successful is moving forward toward a worthy goal.

The feeling of success starts the moment you choose to strive for a worthy goal. Success for you began the moment you chose to read this book. All you need to do now is keep moving forward no matter what. You are a success in this life right now. That I promise you.

Step 5 – Stay Humble

*'True humility is not thinking less of yourself; it is
thinking of yourself less' – C. S. Lewis*

Humility is another key part of our mental, emotional
and spiritual preparation. What does being humble
actually mean and what does it have to do with
fulfillment?

When you start to experience life in the flow, your
circumstances will begin to change and things will just
get automatically easier. It will provide an opening for
your ego to creep back into your life. Softly, at first,
like a whisper you weren't even sure you heard. If your
ego takes hold of your life you could begin to feel a
false sense of confidence and easily slip back into
coveting material things and status again.

From that place where the ego takes hold, what happens
next? More obstacles that will be the lessons you need
to put you back onto the path and get back in touch
with your true self.

Remain humble. It is so easy to fall off of the Soul's
path when we overcome our first obstacles. Our ego
begins to see things it has always craved start to flow to
us naturally and whispers quietly in our mind again.
Once we allow that ego an inch, it will take a mile.
Before we know it, we hit yet another obstacle which is
a warning sign telling us we need to get back in touch
with our Soul pretty quickly.

We are all here in this life by the grace of God. We are
not superior or inferior to anyone else. All of us are
living our lives to learn the lessons that our Soul is

supposed to learn. No life path will be the same.

Step 6 – Embrace Change

'You gain strength, courage, and confidence by every experience in which you really stop to look fear in the face. You must do the thing which you think you cannot do'. - Eleanor Roosevelt

It is imperative for you to overcome your fear of change so you can begin to take positive action.

To help you to make steps towards this, I've included a separate exercise in Appendix D. This exercise takes you through a series of questions to help you consider the consequences of either staying where you are or making the decision to change. It then asks you to consider the effect on your life if you do make changes.

Change feels daunting and that's perfectly natural. Everyone has fear of the unknown. Sometimes that fear is so great that people choose to stay in horrible circumstances instead of moving forward to something, anything else. As an example, let me ask you, can you think of someone who you know who is in or had stayed in an abusive and completely unhealthy relationship for far too long?

Be open to the idea that what you have been looking for may not be what you are meant for. Perhaps that is the reason for the obstacles you have been encountering.

Have you considered that God may be calling you to a different path than the one you are treading right now, and the reason you haven't received it yet is because you are afraid to change?

The obstacles you are consistently encountering may be there to guide you toward a career that is perfectly aligned with your values. It could be a career that up until now you hadn't even considered or didn't even know existed.

Embracing change is not something that can be done in an instant. We can't just swallow a pill so that fear of the unknown magically disappears. It is all part of the process of listening to your Soul. Realize you have been given this life for a reason and understand change will happen, whether you want it to or not. You were not given the blessing of this life so you could sit back and have things be easy. If that were the case you would never grow, never become more.

> *I have noticed even people who claim everything is predestined, and that we can do nothing to change it, look before they cross the road. - Stephen Hawking*

Of course I'm not saying you should be foolish and make immediate and drastic changes without considering the consequences, although that may be exactly what you need. But you can and should take steps every single day in the direction of your desires.

Make no mistake, change will always happen and resistance will only lead to more painful obstacles. The only real question is this, are you going to **make the change, or take the change** that life delivers? Choose to make the bold changes that will create your own beautiful life.

Step 7 – Use Affirmations

"It's the repetition of affirmations that leads to belief. And once that belief becomes a deep conviction, things

> *begin to happen." – Muhammad Ali*

Using affirmations regularly is a great way to program your subconscious mind to believe you are the person who is destined to have all you desire. Your subconscious mind has been slowly programmed over years, particularly during the first few years of your life. For too many of us, our inner beliefs are disempowering.

We become programmed to believe we can't accomplish what we want, or that we are not good enough, or not worthy of what we desire, all of which we have shown to be a completely false belief system. I know you are worthy of what you desire. Here's why.

Because I know God would not allow you to want the things you do, if it wasn't possible. Therefore I know that God wants you to have the things you want too.

Affirmations are specific statements or declarations of things you want to believe. By repeating your affirmations over and over again, with emotion, you will begin to believe your affirmations are true. Using affirmations of the beliefs we want to have is another crucial step toward ensuring you are on the right path to your destination.

So how do you know what affirmations are just right for you? Well the great part is you've already created them. Go back to Exercises 5 and 6 from Chapter 6. Within those answers lie your affirmations.

Exercise 7 – Creating Your Personal Affirmations

We are going to start by looking at the career you have already started to create in the present tense, as if it's already happened. Take the answers that remain in <u>Column 1</u> from Exercise 5 and write them out again in the space below. These are the things you should be thinking of when using the Law of Attraction to manifest your ideal career.

I am so blessed to have and be consistently creating my magnificent career that allows me to:

_____.

_____.

_____.

_____.

_____.

_____.

_____.

_____.

_____.

Before we go any further I want you to repeat what you've just written down out loud. Hearing yourself speak the words will help you begin to believe that these are the new truths about your life.

You now know what a fulfilling career is to your true self. Next we are going to create your personalized affirmations. It's easy because we already know what you value most. Look back at your answers in <u>Column 2</u> from Exercise 6. Insert the answers you kept in the spaces below. These are the way you will feel as you accomplish what is most important to the true you. Take each one of those answers and rewrite them in the blank spaces below:

I am _____.

I am _____.

I am _____.

I am _____.

I am _____.

I am _____.

I am _____.

I am _____.

I am _____.

Read those through slowly.

Now, as before, say them out loud, not with a whisper but with confidence. These are facts. They are truths about you. They are your personal affirmations. Every time you repeat these affirmations, each one of them will program your mind and direct your thoughts, feelings and actions.

And to that I say "Amen" and "Yes you are." *I promise you are – every single affirmation you just spoke out loud – YOU ARE!*

You can state your affirmations any time. Do it as often as possible. In the car on the way to work, in the shower in the morning, or even quietly to yourself while you're waiting in line for coffee. One of the best times to declare your affirmations is before you fall asleep at night. Those moments allow us to enter a state of sleep in a positive state of mind, for our subconscious thoughts to be infused with gratitude and belief rather than anxiety.

Psychological preparation is paramount to put yourself and keep yourself on the right path to your destination. But no matter what, you still have to move your feet.

Chapter Eight – External Directions To Your Destination

*'Inaction breeds doubt and fear. Action breeds
confidence and courage. If you want to conquer fear, do
not sit home and think about it. Go out and get busy.' –
Dale Carnegie*

Move Your Feet

Make no mistake, by making it to this point in the book
you are an amazing and determined person. You have
been through some challenging processes and some soul
searching which is hard to do. If it were easy, everyone
would be doing it. You're embracing change and you're
definitely moving in the direction of the career
fulfillment you deserve.

You now understand why you have not experienced
career fulfillment. You have also taken giant steps down
the path toward understanding who you truly are.
You've recognized the mental and emotional state from
which you will become who you want to be. Our
learning and our state of emerging never really ends, it
simply evolves. Life is one continual learning process, a
process of evolution.

The Quakers have a saying "As you pray, move your
feet." What does that mean? Basically, it means don't
just sit there and expect God to do everything for you. It
means we have to take action too. We have to take
responsibility for our lives and for our attitude. If we
want a miracle, a true transformation in our lives, we
have to create it!

If 80% of your success depends upon your
psychological state and the other 20% depends upon
your mechanics, you've reached the point where 80% of
you is strong and raring to go. Now we are going to look
at the mechanics. The actions you can take, external

directions, starting today to move you in the direction of your desires. No matter how strong your psychology, the life that you want will never drop in to your lap while you're sitting on your couch in your underwear.

I love the story of "The Drowning Man." There was once a man who was stuck on top of his roof in the middle of a huge flood. He was a very spiritual man and he was praying to God for help.

As the spiritual man was busy praying, a man in a rowboat came by and offered to give the man a ride in his rowboat to safety. The spiritual man declined the offer. "No thank you. I am praying to God and he will save me."

Soon after, as the flood waters continued to rise, another man in a motor boat came by and he too offered to give the spiritual man a ride to safety. Again the spiritual man declined the offer. "No thank you, I am praying and God will save me."

Then just as the floodwater was about to wash the spiritual man right off of his roof, a helicopter hovered just over his head. The pilot offered to give the man a ride to safety too, but again the spiritual man declined the offer. "No thank you, God will save me."

Not long after, the floodwaters washed the spiritual man away and he drowned. When he got to heaven he asked God why he did not save him from drowning when he was praying.

God replied, "I sent you a rowboat, a motorboat and a helicopter. What more did you want?"

There is no box that you can pick up at the store that will provide you with a fulfilling career. Happiness and the career of your dreams are things that need to be cultivated over time and as we've already learned, happiness is not a destination, so you will never be able to stop growing and cultivating your perfect career.

Too many people, perhaps even you until now, find it so hard to take any action and make changes even though it is painfully obvious they should. They are afraid; it's a type of fear based paralysis.

Have you ever felt so much anxiety that you did not want to get out of bed in the morning and your fear felt like an enormous weight on your chest? I certainly have. That's precisely when you need to take action the most. There is a wonderful expression I remind myself of all the time.

Doubt takes you out of action, but action takes you out of doubt.

By taking action and facing down your fears, real or imagined, you will immediately gain confidence which will build upon itself. So what do you need to do? How will you move your feet?

Let's get up and get moving.

Keep A Career Journal

"Journal writing is a voyage to the interior." – Christina Baldwin

A perfect place to start taking external steps toward your desires is to keep a career journal. You need to have a place to keep all of your thoughts, feelings and ideas organized. For me the wonderful thing about keeping a career journal is this; I believe once I write down a thought in my journal, it frees up my mind to move on to new thoughts.

A friend of mine once told me, "Sometimes you gotta clean out the fridge to make room for new groceries." That's what my career journal does for me. It gives permanence to my current ideas and emotions so that I don't have to spend energy hanging on to them in my head any longer. Then once they are permanent in my journal, my mind is free to create new ideas and build on old ideas.

It's also a wonderful tool to capture your thinking when life gets so busy and hectic. Sometimes it becomes a challenge to just remember all of your daily responsibilities let alone the things you want to do to create your perfect career. So many of the emotions we feel in the moment or on a particular day are transient. They are fleeting and we quickly forget about them in the challenges of daily living. But these are the emotions we need to capture to understand where we are along the path to career fulfillment and happiness.

Here is another recommendation. I began doing this myself a few months ago. Write down a "Master Career Plan." I update mine at the beginning of every month. I write down exactly how I want my career to progress, what I intend to accomplish in my career and the actions I am taking and will take. Then at the beginning of every month I rewrite my plan again. Even though most of my plan is the same from month to month, it's a great exercise to remind myself of what I want and the direction I want to head toward.

A great place to start to find your "Master Career Plan" would be from the exercises you completed earlier. Look at what a fulfilling career means to you and write them down in your plan. As you write and rewrite your desired destination, ideas will most certainly begin to emerge that will make your destination more specific.

The Decision - Change Your Job or Change Your Mind

"The most difficult thing is the decision to act, the rest is merely tenacity. The fears are paper tigers. You can do anything you decide to do. You can act to change and control your life; and the procedure, the process is its own reward." –Amelia Earhart

You now know what a fulfilled career looks like to you. The question now must be, does your current career situation have the *potential* to be what you are actually looking for? Or, is it time for you to make the decision to act, and make a change?

There is a wonderful short story by Russell H. Conwell entitled "Acres Of Diamonds." It's available as a free download on the internet if you're interested. The story is of a farmer who is tired of the back-breaking work he has to perform every day as a farmer, so he decides to sell his home and farm and go off in search of diamonds and riches.

What happens is the new farmer, the new owner of the land actually discovers diamonds on the property that he purchased. You see the original farmer did not have to leave his farm to find his desire. He was actually sitting on top of "acres of diamonds" all along.

That's what we need to determine next along your

career fulfillment journey. Are you already sitting on your own "acres of diamonds?" Is it possible that your current job is actually your ideal career? Ask yourself this question: 'Can I find an empowering meaning in my career right at this moment?'

What do I mean by an empowering meaning? I mean that within your current career you can realize you are contributing to the greater good and it fits all the criteria of your ideal destination.

The answers we get in life are often a direct result of the questions we ask ourselves.

If you are not fulfilled with your career, you are most likely continually clinging to dissatisfaction. When nurturing unhappiness, you are likely asking yourself what it is you *don't* like about your current job. Let's flip that over now and look at things in a different way.

Ask yourself the following question: What could you consider to be great about your career right now – today? Perhaps it's your work colleagues who support you when things get tough, whether at work or at home? Is there one particular aspect of your job that really makes you feel alive, such as customer satisfaction, analyzing data, working on certain projects?

If you are either unemployed or underemployed, what are the positive aspects about your current situation? Does the free time give you the opportunity to take on some volunteer work and touch someone's life in a way you would never be able if you were working? Are you considering retraining for new skills to broaden your career options, taking your journey in a new and better direction?

There are always positive angles to every career situation we find ourselves in. It's often a case of reframing the way we look at things. What is great about your career situation right NOW? Think of and write down at least 5 things about your current career you can be grateful for.

Perhaps all you need to do is to look at your current career circumstances in a new and positive light. It's like the child who is raised in a town where their parents lived and possibly their grandparents too. They vow to escape as soon as they are old enough to leave but when they do they miss home! They begin to understand that they had focused only on the negative aspects of their environment and overlooked everything that was good about it.

Ultimately, they admit to themselves that the old town where they were raised is where they want to be. They like all the people and know the back streets like the back of their hand. They have seen their town change and evolve over the years. They realize – that place is home. So they go home.

Is that you? Could your current working environment reflect that situation for you? I'm not saying it is. What I'm saying is you need to consider all options before you make the decision to change your job or career. If your current career is not in sync with your destination, then you will ultimately need to make a career change. Perhaps just having a new perspective will allow you to stay where you are long enough to find the next step on you career fulfillment journey.

If you know for sure you need to make changes to your job in order to have career fulfillment there's one essential thing you must do – NOW. Remember the 'attitude of gratitude'. Before you begin to make any changes, you have to appreciate where you are today, no matter what. When you begin to look at your current working environment in a positive light and feel grateful for where you are *at this very moment of your life*, then the changes you so deeply desire will flow into your life.

If you are currently out of work or underemployed you may be wondering how on earth you are going to find the positive spin on where your career is today. When it seems as though there is nothing to be grateful for and no light at the end of the tunnel, one thing is certain, nature is on your side. Nature abhors a vacuum. Wherever nature sees an empty space, it will get filled.

Think about it for a moment and it will make perfect sense. When you clean up your desk, how long does it take for the mess to accumulate again and it looks the same as it did before you cleaned it? Try digging a hole in your yard (not literally right now, unless you need a hole of course!) How long will it take before the grass and weeds begin to grow in and fill that hole?

Your career needs room to grow. Accept the space in your life and see how nature fills it with something brand new for you. Don't fight to hang on to what once was. Embrace nature's process; embrace the hole in your career and expect good things to flow into it.

Also if you are unemployed or underemployed, a new way to approach your career search is to stop looking for a job at all. Don't look for a job, look for meaningful work. There is a difference.

Think about the job you would really love to be doing. Is there a way of volunteering for that position? Voluntary work will not only be rewarding, but you may very well find that new doors of opportunity will begin to open for you as you experience gratitude for what you are doing.

Don't sit home complaining to anyone who will listen about the lack of response to all of the resumes you've sent out to prospective employers. Don't surf the net analyzing all of the daunting statistics about unemployment and the numbers of applicants applying for each job in an attempt to justify your current predicament. Put your lap top down now. Get out there; find those organizations that need help in areas in which you would love to work. Find something that fits your destination.

Whatever your decision, you must decide. You know what the right answer is already. Stay in your current job and simply change your thinking, because your current job fits your destination already? Stay in your current job and be grateful now and use it as a bridge to your next opportunity? Or make sweeping changes right now? The answer lies within you. Use your career journal to process and write out your conclusion.

Giving Is Empowering

"You can get everything in life you want if you will just help enough other people get what they want." – Zig Ziglar

When we are experiencing an unfulfilling career, we feel a sense of lacking what we want. Subconsciously we are thinking about what we don't have and that feeling of lack causes us to hold on as tightly as we can to what we have, including our time.

I once read that the most successful people were also generally the biggest givers. Makes sense right? I thought so. I thought that once I was successful I would be a better giver too. Heck, I was looking forward to it. But what if it doesn't work that way? What if giving is a pathway to success and not a by-product of success?

The next time you leave your home, just see how simple it is to help someone else, to *give* to anyone, even a complete stranger. Here are some ideas to get you thinking:

- Smile at anyone but preferably a stranger. Genuinely smile, use your eyes! Smile at them until they have to smile back at you.

- Hold open a door to allow people through.

- Pay someone – anyone – an unsolicited compliment about their hair, the way they dress or, if at work, for something they've done where they've really made an effort to do their best.

- Mow the lawn of an elderly neighbor who struggles to do it for himself.

- Ask someone how they are feeling and genuinely mean it. Don't just wait for the 'fine thanks', ask them 'how are YOU' and allow them time to truly respond. If they are having a bad time, listen and empathize, ask them if there's anything you can do to help. You may find that the simple act of listening is more than enough.

You don't have to wait to achieve your dreams before you give. It doesn't work that way. Don't get the order wrong. By giving you will actually become more successful in your career. What goes around comes around.

Now let me point out that if you give, and then immediately look around to see if your career is improving – that is not giving. That's you trying to barter with the universe. Give to give, give joyfully, give without expecting anything in return but most importantly, *give from the heart.*

The absolute fastest way out of your problems is to help someone else with theirs. I promise you. Here are a few more examples of ways that you can give and take your mind off of your own circumstances.

- The next time you see someone whose car has broken down, stop and help them push it to a safe place. Be that Good Samaritan; don't pass by on the other side of the road.

- Let someone who feels alone and scared know that you are there for them and they are not alone.

- Visit someone who is in the hospital to see if there is anything they need before they are ready to go home. Find out how they are getting home.

Remember, you are a divine creation and God can work through you any time you allow it to happen. I challenge you to make a difference, to contribute to making the world a better place in some small yet meaningful way.

'No one has ever become poor by giving.' Anne Frank

Make the world a better place in some way. Here are just a few benefits of giving:

- **You feel better**. In volunteering to help others, you are passing on a wonderful gift. First of all, your time – what is more precious than that, after all? Secondly, all of those things in your life that you are so grateful for, all of those blessings are being passed to others. You'll more than likely want to do it again because of the feelings of joy and gratitude it gives you.

- **Improved self-esteem and confidence.** People who help those who are less fortunate than themselves feel a sense of increased confidence and self-esteem. You're virtually guaranteed a positive response from others for helping them and they'll begin to see you in a new light. Ultimately, you will begin to see you in a new light too.

- **You attract good things into your life.** We've already talked about the Law of Attraction. In order to attract good into our lives we have to feel positive emotions for ourselves. Just remember, you should be giving without thought of receiving. God knows your heart.

- **You're giving out positive energy.** Let's face it, who would you rather spend your time with? Someone who smiles all the time or someone who sports a habitual frown? Positive actions and positive attitudes are attractive. It's as simple as that.

- **You'll be making a difference.** You'll be contributing to the greater good which is fulfilling to your Soul.

- **You'll forget that negative outlook.**
  Subconsciously you'll feel as if you are coming
  from a place of HAVING and not lacking.

These words from the Dalai Lama capture the essence
of this section:

*"I believe that the very purpose of life is to be happy.
From the very core of our being, we desire contentment.
In my own limited experience I have found that the more
we care for the happiness of others, the greater is our
own sense of well-being. Cultivating a close,
warmhearted feeling for others automatically puts the
mind at ease. It helps remove whatever fears or
insecurities we may have and gives us the strength to
cope with any obstacles we encounter. It is the principal
source of success in life. Since we are not solely material
creatures, it is a mistake to place all our hopes for
happiness on external development alone. The key is to
develop inner peace."*

Staying Healthy

*"To keep the body in good health is a duty... otherwise
we shall not be able to keep our mind strong and clear." -
Buddha*

The focus of this book isn't on health and fitness or
nutrition. However, trying to maintain a sensible diet
with good nutrition combined with adequate levels of
physical exercise can be a tremendous boost to being
content in your job or career.

All I'd say to you is, don't neglect your physical health.
There's a wealth of information available on how to
maintain a regular exercise pattern and a healthy diet
online.

Recently Steve Jobs, the former CEO of Apple Inc. passed away from cancer. Not many people have ever achieved as much success in business as Jobs did. On his death bed, do you think he would have traded all of his success for more time with his family? More time to connect and contribute and love? I don't know but I would think so. Let's not take our health for granted.

Also, exercise is a great way to keep anxiety at bay. It helps to promote a good night's sleep and it's a great time to allow your mind to drift and think of new ideas to grow and advance your life and career.

Meet With People Often – Networking Pays

Great minds discuss ideas; average minds discuss events; small minds discuss people. - Eleanor Roosevelt

To help broaden and solidify your thoughts and feelings about your career, as well as the actions you are taking to create a fulfilling career, you must meet with people regularly. Discuss your ideas and get other people's ideas as well. You can gain insight from anyone who is positive and thoughtful.

Meet with as many people as possible who already have the type of career fulfillment that you seek. Perhaps they work in the field that interests you and perhaps not. Both can be helpful. When you meet find out how they became successful and ask them for advice on how you can get there. You'll be surprised to find out how willing most people are to help or at least point you in the right direction.

Meet with friends and current or former colleagues who you feel comfortable discussing your career plans with. In this type of meeting you can be a bit more open about your feelings and brainstorm about career options. Encourage them to be honest with you and in turn do the same for them. You may well find they are in a similar situation to you. If they are, help them out. Tell them to read this book!

Meet with people through professional associations in your area. Set up meetings with new people you can brainstorm with about career advancement and fulfillment. People search for the word "career" on Google over 83 million times globally each month and there are dozens of variations to the search for "career" that account for millions more. You are not at all alone in your desire to have a fulfilling career. It won't be hard to find people to meet with and share ideas about career fulfillment, you just need to start looking and they'll be there.

Another place to look for networking partners is through social media. LinkedIn is a great site for professionals to broaden their professional reach and find their next career move. Join groups and make connections with influential people. You should highlight your achievements and your qualifications. Use keywords that allow recruiters in your field to *find you*. Connect with those recruiters too. In Appendix E I've included a guide on how to get started on LinkedIn and begin to build up your own network – that's if you haven't already.

Meet just to meet. Every meeting will bring out a new idea. Meet with new people and meet regularly with the same people. Building your network is vital. It may not bring instant career openings but further down the line you may well find you're connected to someone who can be a great help to you.

You can probably think of at least 5 people that would be worthwhile for you to meet with. Write their names down now. Use your career journal if you've started it already. Then take some action. By the end of the next business day set up meetings with 2 of the people you listed. Meet for coffee, meet for lunch, just meet.

Eliminate Time Thieves

Finally you may have been wondering when, exactly, I was expecting you to actually *do* all of these things. When are you going to have the time to - manifest, use your affirmations, write in your career journal, give of yourself and your time, exercise and last but not least, meet with people often?

My guess is, one of the often repeated excuses you make as to why you aren't taking steps today to move towards your career destination is you simply don't have the time. There are only so many hours in the day! I'm only one person! I've only got 2 hands! I can't make more time! Or, can you? Let's take a look at that now and figure out where we can make time.

Do you use time to do any of the following?

- Watch mindless television every night.

- Spend too much time in bars.

- Scroll through Facebook so you can see what someone you went to kindergarten with had for breakfast.

- Aimlessly surf the web.

- Shop. Ladies?

- Spend time with negative people. People who
  suck all the positive energy out of the room.
  They are miserable, they want to stay that way,
  and they want to convince you to be that way
  too.

Perhaps you can think of a few other examples of ways
in which you spend time doing things that are not at all
constructive.

On top of that, I want you to think about how many
hours you spend traveling to work each week. That is all
time that you can use positively and may inadvertently
waste. If you're stuck in a car or on a train you can't
actually be doing anything else physically but there is an
abundance of positive audio books available. Rather
than listen to constant news reports on all that's wrong
with the world that fill your mind with more negative
thoughts, try listening to an audio CD or book that will
allow you to learn and grow.

If you were to only listen to a Self-Improvement audio
book in your car for 15 minutes a day Monday through
Friday for a year it would add up to 65 HOURS of time
you will be flooding your mind with strong,
transformational, positive ideas.

Your commute may be more than 15 minutes each day!
If you do a quick calculation of your time you'll
probably find it's in excess of 65 hours. Think of all of
those positive messages feeding your mind and
transforming those previously negative thought patterns.

It can seem a bit daunting to try and figure out where to

start when selecting which audio books and audio programs to choose so I made it easier for you by adding a "recommended resources" section to the website www.careerfulfillmentfound.com.

It's often said that it takes only thirty days to create a new habit. Make this one of your first new habits.

Exercise 8 – Time Thieves

Write down five things you do at night when you get home from work which are not constructive. Then write down another 5 things you spend time doing on the weekends that are not constructive.

Weeknights

1..

2..

3..

4..

5..

Weekends

1..

2..

3..

4..

5...

Exercise 9 – Take Action

Your final exercise is to take a moment and write down a handful of activities that come to mind right now which will help you achieve the happiness and career fulfillment you deserve. For example, who can you get in touch with for advice on your career? What research can you do online? Who can you arrange meetings with? Do you have a LinkedIn profile? Do you have your Career Journal?

1. _____

2. _____

3. _____

4. _____

5. _____

6. _____

7. _____

8. _____

9. _____

10. _____

Follow through and take consistent and constant action.

Conclusion

Now

Now move forward. Move confidently with a sense of positive expectation. You've earned it. Knowing what you know now, what *can't* you accomplish? You know:

- Happiness and a successful career are not destinations. They are states of being which you can choose for yourself.

- You must BE happy to achieve happiness.

- The flow of happiness, contentment and gratitude is the state you are meant to be in.

- The authentic you is exactly who you must be to find fulfillment. You are just right.

- You are not your ego. You are a beautiful spirit. You have come from God and one day will return to God.

- Fulfillment is found in giving, loving, growth and connection.

- What you look for, you will find.

- The answers you receive are a direct result of the questions you ask.

- The Universe is there to help you achieve your desires.

- Obstacles are lessons for growth. All that you are experiencing is exactly what you need to grow.

- One day you will realize it was not necessary to worry about everything you are worrying about now.

- Your ideal destination. What you want to have and do. Who you want to be.

- Internal and external directions to your destination.

- You *are* successful right now.

Again I ask, what *can't* you accomplish?

Continue to learn and grow. Keep your eyes open for new "teachers." Self improvement is a never ending process.

Recall the chapter where we discussed lifting weights to strengthen muscle. What results do you think you would achieve if you were to go to the gym just one time? You'd be awfully sore for a week but you wouldn't make any physical improvements from trying just once. You have to be consistent. You have to keep going to become stronger.

The same principle applies to your relationships. What if you were to tell your significant other "I love you" just one time? Will that last forever? Of course it won't. You need to work on relationships. You must continually show and reinforce love.

Make growth a part of who you are. You might as well make an effort to improve, because if you don't God will insist that you work just to stay the same. You know what you need to do.

You

You are truly a unique individual who cares enough to take time and put forth the effort to improve. In this life, that does in fact make you remarkable. My prayer for you is that you accept the happiness and career fulfillment you are meant to have into your life.

Of course there will be times when you get knocked off the path. You're human and emotions can sneak up on you. Put the lessons you've learned in this book to work every day as well as the new lessons you will learn going forward. Do that, and without question you will experience happiness and career fulfillment.

Never stop trying and you will never know failure.

I promise you, your life matters. God knows it too. Believe it and make it so every single day of this life. Fighting and clamoring for certainty will not bring you certainty. Fighting and clamoring for importance will not make you important. Strive every day to matter, in small ways, and you will become important and you will know certainty.

Wonderful changes are already in place and I couldn't be happier for you.

APPENDIX A

EXERCISE

Circle the words on this paper to reflect who you feel
*you **can be** within your working environment*

Loving   Dynamic   Kind   Caring   Encouraging

Compassionate   Team Leader   Sympathetic

Communication Skills – Written

Communication Skills – Verbal   Presentation Skills

Organized   Diligent   Self-Motivated

Inspirational   Pace Setter   Goal Oriented

Disciplined   Serious   Thoughtful   Considerate

Entrepreneurial   Hard Working   Spontaneous

Coaching   Team Player   Manager   Creative

Quick Thinking   Articulate   Patient   Diplomatic

Tactful   Ethical   Genuine   Fair   Loyal   Critical

Thinking   Strategic   Negotiator

APPENDIX B

Ego Vs Soul

Courtesy of Justine Musk

The ego is about image.
The soul is about authenticity.

The ego can't take constructive criticism.
The soul seeks it out and welcomes it.

The ego confuses itself with the work..
The soul stands apart from the work.

The ego wants to be seen as the best.
The soul wants to keep getting better.

The ego is about the number of fans and followers.
The soul is about relatedness and community.

The ego wants to be famous.
The soul wants to start a movement.

The ego is all about me.
The soul promotes self through serving others.

The ego tries to control the message.
The soul trusts the message to take on a life of its own.

The ego talks.
The soul looks and listens.

The ego is closed off.
The soul is open and transparent.

The ego competes and dominates.
The soul co-creates.

The ego lives from scarcity.
The soul lives from abundance.

The ego cares only about the end performance.
The soul is in love with the process.

The ego contracts.
The soul expands.

The ego is spam.
The soul is useful content.

The ego is hollow.
The soul contains multitudes.

APPENDIX C

Tips on Meditation

Courtesy of The Conscious Life

Choose a conducive environment. Find a nice, quiet place where you won't be disturbed for fifteen minutes or longer. Sit down, relax and rest your hands on your lap. You can sit on the floor cross-legged with the support of a meditation cushion, or on any chair with your feet resting on the ground. It's not necessary to force yourself into a lotus position if you're not used to it.

Regardless of how you sit, it's important to maintain the natural curve of your back. That means, no slouching.

Breathe slowly and deeply. Close your eyes softly. Begin by taking a few slow and deep breaths — inhaling with your nose and exhaling from your mouth. Don't force your breathing. Let it come naturally. The first few intakes of air are likely to be shallow, but as you allow more air to fill your lungs each time, your breaths will gradually become deeper and fuller. Take as long as you need to breathe slowly and deeply.

Be aware. When you are breathing deeply, you'll begin to feel calmer and more relaxed. That's a good sign. Now, focus your attention on your breathing. Be aware of each breath that you take in through your nose. Be mindful of each breath that you exhale with your mouth. Continue focusing on your breaths for as long as you like.

If you find your attention straying away from your breaths, just gently bring it back. It may happen many times. Don't be disheartened. What's important is to realize that you've wandered and bring your attention back to where it should be. As you develop greater focus power, you will find it easier to concentrate.

Ending the session. When you are ready to end the session, open your eyes and stand up slowly. Stretch yourself and extend your increased awareness to your next activities. Well done! You've done it!

Meditation Tips for Beginners

Guided meditation MP3s or CDs as meditation tools. For beginners, audio guided meditations provide step-by-step instructions that help to introduce meditation in an easy and non-intimidating way.

Experienced meditators may also benefit from guided meditation programs as they can reveal different perspectives and approaches that might have escaped one's awareness.

Aim to have the length of your exhales as long, if not longer, than your inhales. By expelling more used air, you make more room for fresh air to fill your lungs. If your out-breaths are much shorter than the in-breaths, you can help to expel more air by gently contracting your abdominal muscles.

If the weather is chilly, keep yourself warm with a blanket or shawl during meditation.

Meditating with an empty or full stomach may be

distracting or even uncomfortable. Make sure there's something in your tummy, but not so much that you feel distracted while sitting.

Some people find it easier to meditate with light music in the background, while others prefer total silence. If you belong to the first group, choose appropriate tunes that help you to calm down and yet won't distract you from your practice. Some examples are sounds of nature (such as ocean waves), traditional music (such as Native American music) as well as contemporary meditation music. The choice of music, or lack of, is entirely a matter of personal preference. So feel free to experiment and see what works best for you.

Use a meditation timer or any countdown timer. It tells you your time is up without you having to think about it constantly. You can use the timer that's built into your mobile phone or digital watch.

Once you've mastered breathing meditation, you can choose to continue with it or try other meditation techniques. There are many types of meditation techniques that can help you to develop inner qualities which you never know existed.

APPENDIX D

OVERCOMING THE FEAR OF CHANGE[1]

Here are the questions to ask yourself to understand the consequences of remaining where you are:

1. What will it cost me in my life if I continue living this way?

2. What is the ultimate consequence?

3. What will it cost me emotionally, in my relationships, friendships, family, finances, health, spiritual life?

4. What will I have to give up or miss out on by living this way?

5. What have I already missed out on? What has it already cost me in my life?

6. What will it cost me 5 years, 10 years, 15 years, 20 years from now if I continue living this way?

Alternatively, you can also ask positive questions to see how the changes you make will positively enhance your life:

1. What will I gain by doing this?

2. How is this going to move me closer towards my dreams and who I want to become?

3. How will doing this add to every area of my

life? My relationships? Emotional life? Finances? Health? etc…

4. What will my life be like 5, 10, 15, 20 years from now by doing this?

Consistently ask yourself these questions throughout the day.

The truth will set you free.

1 *With thanks to projectlifemastery.com*

APPENDIX E

A BRIEF GUIDE TO GETTING STARTED ON LINKEDIN

LinkedIn is extremely useful to everyone wanting to establish themselves in their career or for those wanting a career move.

Setting Up A Profile

If you don't have a LinkedIn profile, visit www.linkedin.com and sign up immediately. Creating a basic profile is free and it's sufficient for most needs.

You'll find LinkedIn's New User Starter Guide (http://learn.linkedin.com/new-users) within their Learning Center extremely comprehensive but the following tips are also useful to note:

- Always include a photograph, preferably a professional one.

- Do not include confidential information, this is a public domain.

- Utilize all of the features that you possibly can to create a comprehensive profile, particularly when it comes to skillsets. This gives you the opportunity to include keywords for the jobs you are interested in (or for recruiters to find you).

- Update your profile regularly so potential contacts and employers see you are active.

- As you become established and create a network, ask for recommendations. LinkedIn also launched a new endorsements (http://blog.linkedin.com/2012/09/24/introducin g-endorsements-give-kudos-with-just-one-click) feature which makes it easier to gain approval from your LinkedIn network.

- Make use of all of the relevant plug-ins and apps that may be useful for you personally.

- Make use of the summary box to describe who you are, not just the job that you do.

- All of your notable career achievements and qualifications should be included but must match the detail on your resume.

- Join relevant groups. It's an ideal way to network, establish new connections and keep updated with opportunities in the industries you are interested in.

- Make connections. Always include a covering note with your request to connect explaining why you are requesting a connection (for example, a shared group).

About the Author

Jason Hyde has figured something out and he wants to share it with you. Jason became a passionate student of all things related to self improvement in 2006 after a difficult period in his life. A financial services industry professional, Jason has figured out how to have and keep a truly fulfilling career. He lives in southern Connecticut with his wife and two young sons. Feel free to contact Jason at Jason@careerfulfillmentfound.com